Biography Today

Profiles of People of Interest to Young Readers

Volume 21
Issue 1
January 2012

Cherie D. Abbey
Managing Editor

Omnigraphics

155 W. Congress
Suite 200
Detroit, MI 48226

Cherie D. Abbey, *Managing Editor*

Peggy Daniels, Joan Goldsworthy, Kevin Hillstrom, Laurie Hillstrom, Justin Karr, Leslie Karr, and Diane Telgen, *Sketch Writers*

Allison A. Beckett and Mary Butler, *Research Staff*

* * *

Peter E. Ruffner, *Publisher*
Matthew P. Barbour, *Senior Vice President*

* * *

Elizabeth Collins, *Research and Permissions Coordinator*
Kevin M. Hayes, *Operations Manager*
Cherry Stockdale, *Permissions Assistant*

Shirley Amore, Joseph Harris, Martha Johns, and Kirk Kauffmann, *Administrative Staff*

Special thanks to Frederick G. Ruffner for creating this series.

Copyright © 2012 EBSCO Publishing, Inc.
ISSN 1058-2347 • ISBN 978-0-7808-1253-6

Library of Congress Cataloging-in-Publication Data

Contents

Preface

Biography Today is a magazine designed and written for the young reader—ages 9 and above—and covers individuals that librarians and teachers tell us that young people want to know about most: entertainers, athletes, writers, illustrators, cartoonists, and political leaders.

The Plan of the Work

The publication was especially created to appeal to young readers in a format they can enjoy reading and readily understand. Each issue contains approximately 10 sketches arranged alphabetically. Each entry provides at least one picture of the individual profiled, and boldfaced rubrics lead the reader to information on birth, youth, early memories, education, first jobs, marriage and family, career highlights, memorable experiences, hobbies, and honors and awards. Each of the entries ends with a list of easily accessible sources designed to lead the student to further reading on the individual and a current address. Retrospective entries are also included, written to provide a perspective on the individual's entire career.

Biographies are prepared by Omnigraphics editors after extensive research, utilizing the most current materials available. Those sources that are generally available to students appear in the list of further reading at the end of the sketch.

Indexes

Cumulative indexes are an important component of *Biography Today*. Each issue of the *Biography Today* General Series includes a Cumulative Names Index, which comprises all individuals profiled in *Biography Today* since the series began in 1992. In addition, we compile three other indexes: the Cumulative General Index, Places of Birth Index, and Birthday Index. See our web site, www.biographytoday.com, for these three indexes, along with the Names Index. All *Biography Today* indexes are cumulative, including all individuals profiled in both the General Series and the Subject Series.

Our Advisors

This series was reviewed by an Advisory Board comprising librarians, children's literature specialists, and reading instructors to ensure that the concept of this publication—to provide a readable and accessible biographical magazine for young readers—was on target. They evaluated the title as it developed, and their suggestions have proved invaluable. Any errors, however, are ours alone. We'd like to list the Advisory Board members and to thank them for their efforts.

Our Advisory Board stressed to us that we should not shy away from controversial or unconventional people in our profiles, and we have tried to follow their advice. The Advisory Board also mentioned that the sketches might be useful in reluctant reader and adult literacy programs, and we would value any comments librarians might have about the suitability of our magazine for those purposes.

Your Comments Are Welcome

Our goal is to be accurate and up to date, to give young readers information they can learn from and enjoy. Now we want to know what you think. Take a look at this issue of *Biography Today*, on approval. Contact me with your comments. We want to provide an excellent source of biographical information for young people. Let us know how you think we're doing.

Cherie Abbey
Managing Editor, *Biography Today*
Omnigraphics, Inc.
155 W. Congress, Suite 200
Detroit, MI 48226
www.omnigraphics.com
editorial@omnigraphics.com

Congratulations!

Congratulations to the following individuals and libraries who are receiving a free copy of *Biography Today*, Vol. 21, No. 1, for suggesting people who appear in this issue.

Annie Curtis, Gallatin Pulbic Library, Gallatin, TN

Paul Dicken, Aurora Elementary School, Dillsboro Elementary School, Moores Hill Elementary School, South Dearborn Community Schools, Aurora, IN

Rebecca Foster, Memorial Pathway Academy, Garland, TX

Orie Ramos, Lakewood Public Schools, Sunfield, MI

Shreya Subramanian, Martell Elementary School, Troy, MI

Sharon Thackston, Gallatin Public Library, Gallatin, TN

Sierra M. Yoder, Shipshewana, IN

Rob Bell 1970-

American Religious Leader, Author, Speaker, and Founding Pastor of the Mars Hill Bible Church

BIRTH

Robert Holmes Bell Jr., known as Rob, was born on August 23, 1970, in Ingham County, Michigan. He grew up in Okemos, not far from Michigan's capital, Lansing. His parents are Helen and Robert Holmes Bell. He has a brother, Jonathan, and a sister, Ruth.

YOUTH

Bell's father was a judge in Michigan's Ingham District Court and the Ingham County Circuit Court. In 1987, he was nominated to the U.S. District Court by then-president Ronald Reagan and confirmed for the position by the U.S. Senate. The Bell children grew up in a household where they were challenged to think deeply and critically. Dinner was not just a time for eating, but was also a time for meaningful conversation among the family. The parents expected their children to read certain books, including the fiction and nonfiction of C. S. Lewis, author of the "Narnia" series. Lewis's writing frequently explores Christian themes.

> *"My parents were intellectually rigorous," Bell remembered. "Ask questions, explore, don't take things at face value. Stretch. I've always been interested in the thing behind the thing."*

The Bells raised their children with conservative Christian values and beliefs, but they didn't discourage them from challenging those beliefs. "My parents were intellectually rigorous," Bell remembered. "Ask questions, explore, don't take things at face value. Stretch. I've always been interested in the thing behind the thing."

Bell's father remembered that even when his son was only about 10 years old, he demonstrated an unusual interest in, and understanding of, people and their problems. "There he'd be, riding along with me, ... going to see sick folks or friends who were having problems, and he would get back in the truck after a visit and begin to analyze them and their situation very acutely. He had a feel for people and how they felt from very early on."

EDUCATION

Bell graduated from Okemos High School in 1988. He then enrolled at Wheaton College, a highly ranked, private, Christian, liberal arts school located just west of Chicago, Illinois. Unsure about what he really wanted to do with his life, Bell decided to major in psychology, but his main interest was music. He sang and played guitar in a rock band called ___ ton bundle, an alt-rock group whose guitar player dressed as a pirate. The band's name starts with an underlined space that was filled in with words that changed from time to time. "Rapunzel ton bundle" and "nun ton bundle" were two examples Bell remembered.

Bell has admitted that he was not an outstanding musician, but that didn't dampen his enthusiasm. "What I lack in talent, I make up in volume and passion," he said. He had always felt he had a lot of creative energy, but he didn't know what to do with it until he started playing with the band. Performing was a lot of fun, and it taught him to express himself,

Rob with his baby brother.

"writing and playing, working with words and images and metaphors. You might say the music unleashed a monster," he reflected. Being in a rock band might seem an unlikely way to prepare for a career as a church pastor, but both require "taking a statement, crafting it, delivering it," Bell explained. "Something was birthed there. It was all a warm-up for the first time I ever preached."

At that time, however, Bell still had no thought of becoming a pastor, or any other ideas about his life path other than making music with ___ ton bundle. The band was moderately successful, playing in clubs around the Chicago area; but during Bell's senior year at Wheaton, ___ ton bundle fell apart, for various reasons. Bell became seriously ill with viral meningitis, a life-threatening inflammation of the tissues around the brain. His recovery required a long stay in the hospital, and by the time he was ready to play again, ___ ton bundle's guitarist had moved on to study at a seminary. The band never came back together.

In 1992, Bell graduated with a Bachelor of Arts (BA) degree. That summer, he worked as a water-skiing instructor at Honey Rock Camp, which is run by Wheaton College. One day, when no one else was available, Bell was asked to preach a message to a group of counselors. This spur-of-the-moment experience transformed his life. "I thought, 'This is what I'm supposed to do,'" he recalled. Other people had already suggested to him that he should consider being a pastor, but he had never agreed with them. Now he believed it was his calling, and he enrolled at the Fuller Theological Seminary, a Protestant divinity school in Pasadena, California.

Bell wanted to be a pastor, but he knew he'd always do things a little differently than the norm. He wanted his ministry to be "vibrant and subversive," and he constantly searched for creative new ways to get his points across. His efforts did not earn him good grades, but he did complete his master of divinity degree. During his time at Fuller, he worked as a youth intern at the Lake Avenue Church in Pasadena. He also got some new

Rob with his band, __ton bundle.

ideas about how worship services might be conducted when he and his wife Kristen, whom he had met while at Wheaton, attended Christian Assembly, a progressive church in Eagle Rock.

FIRST JOBS

Following his graduation from Fuller, Bell was invited to be an intern at Calvary Church in Grand Rapids, Michigan. Like Lake Avenue Church and Christian Assembly, Calvary Church falls into the "megachurch" category, meaning the weekly attendance averages more than 2,000 people. At the time of Bell's internship, Calvary was under the direction of Reverend Ed Dobson, who had became well known as one of the leaders of the Moral Majority, a political action group that lobbied on behalf of conservative causes.

Soon Bell had taken over the Saturday night services at Calvary, which had a more casual, modern feel than the Sunday morning service. He was popular, but he wasn't satisfied. He kept looking for new ways to present the Bible and its message. One of his goals was to reach people who might be uncomfortable at a traditional church service. "Most understandings of preaching/teaching have a whole bunch of fundamental assumptions about how it's done," he argued. "You are fitting truth into a prescribed format—generally, a person standing behind a podium, reading the Bible and talking. And so the deepest truths of the universe then are going to need to get run through a very narrow funnel." Bell felt very strongly that "there was a whole generation of people hungry for Jesus, but unable to connect with the churches they had experienced." In 1998, this feeling led him to start a totally new church group. He had "a defining moment" when he realized "If nobody comes, it's still a success. Because we tried something new."

CAREER HIGHLIGHTS

Founding Mars Hill Bible Church

Bell decided to call his new church Mars Hill Bible Church. Like Calvary Church, it would be nondenominational. This means that while its members identify themselves as Christians, the church is not part of any officially organized branch of Christianity. The name refers to a hill near Athens, Greece, known as the Areopagus, or Mars Hill. It was the site of an altar dedicated to "an unknown god," a figure that represented all the gods not known or recognized in the Greek pantheon. It is recorded in the Bible that upon seeing this altar, Paul, one of the Apostles of Jesus, proclaimed: "What you worship as something unknown I am going to proclaim to you. The God who made the world and everything in it is the Lord of heaven and earth and does not live in temples built by hands."

—— " ——

"Jesus is more compelling than ever," Bell has said. "More inviting, more true, more mysterious than ever. The problem isn't Jesus; the problem is what comes with Jesus."

—— " ——

The first meetings of the Mars Hill Bible Church were held in February 1999, in a school gym in Wyoming, Michigan. More than 1,000 people showed up at the church's first worship service. The group soon began meeting in a large warehouse space owned by a church member, with some 4,000 people visiting each week. They were drawn in by Pastor Bell's energetic, casual, humorous style; his youthful, modern mindset; and the upbeat music used in worship.

Numbers continued to swell, and within a year, the congregation was preparing to move to a much larger, permanent location. A benefactor had given Mars Hill an abandoned shopping mall in nearby Grandville. Funds were raised to buy the land around the building, and the space that had formerly served as the mall's main store was converted into a place for worship. The first services were held there in July 2000. Church member-

Bell has often taken his message on the road,
as in this sermon in Ann Arbor, Michigan.

ship grew very rapidly, and by 2005, an estimated 11,000 people attended services at Mars Hill each week. Some 30,000 more visited the church's web site to watch Bell's sermons and downloaded them and other features.

Bell's intense attitude towards his work was summed up in his statement: "A good sermon will exhaust and inspire you.... You'll say 'Whoa—that's a full meal. It'll take me a week to recover from that.'" During this period of explosive growth at Mars Hill, however, he did much more than merely write and deliver dynamic sermons. He threw himself into every aspect of running the church and serving the congregation.

Eventually, the hectic pace and the demands of being spiritual leader to so many people took their toll. One Sunday morning, about five years after the church got started, Bell found himself hiding in a storage room at the church shortly before his 11:00 service. He was afraid to face the crowd and wondering what would happen if he ran for his car at that moment and drove away as fast as he could. He didn't go through with his fantasies of escape, but he did visit his doctor, who told him he was badly overworked and needed a break.

Bell took 10 weeks off, spending much of that time alone and in the outdoors. Upon reflection, he said that one of the things he needed to do at that point was to get past the feeling that he had to prove himself. He returned to Mars Hill, but turned most of the pastor's duties over to other people. He focused his own energies on his sermons and writing. Bell also vowed to make every Friday a kind of retreat day, on which he disconnects from technology—cell phone, e-mail, and social networking sites—and focuses on things other than his work.

Reaching Out to the World

One aspect many people find appealing about Mars Hill is its emphasis on making a real difference in the world, both locally and globally. The church has a mentoring program designed to help the inner-city youth of Grand Rapids. The church also helps refugee families who are starting new lives in Michigan make the adjustment to their new home and its culture. Mars Hill also participates in programs to bring clean water to underprivileged areas in the African country of Rwanda, and it supports a program that makes small-business loans available to people in need around the world. It is typical of the church's priorities that they have continued to meet in their no-frills setting—the old shopping mall—rather than investing funds in a new church building.

"[Bell has] figured out how to convey basic Christian doctrine in a highly skeptical culture," said Quentin J. Schultze, a professor of communication at Calvin College. "He's very challenging in his sermons. There's no appeal for money. You get a sense of intellectual substance and depth of the faith."

Bell spreads the Mars Hill message in other ways, too. The church, like many megachurches, makes extensive use of modern technology. Many people download Mars Hill podcasts and access other features the church makes available through the Internet. Music and inspirational CDs are also available for purchase on the church's web site. The church's basic message of acceptance for all is summed up in the bumper stickers given away after each service, which state simply: "LOVE WINS."

Writing books provided another way for Bell to reach people. His first was *Velvet Elvis: Repainting the Christian Faith,* published in 2005. Its title came from an old ___ ton bundle song, "Velvet Elvis." The themes in the book are closely related to the ideas that inspired Bell to found Mars Hill Bible

Church. The book is aimed at people who feel drawn to Jesus Christ, but who have difficulties dealing with traditional religious worship. Bell states that Christianity needs to be continually re-imagined and re-invented. He feels that this keeps Christianity from becoming stuck in outdated traditions and stagnant systems. As Cindy Crosby wrote in *Christianity Today,* "Joy, awe, raw honesty, and an appreciation for the mystery of faith permeate the pages." Another reviewer, James D. Davis, wrote in the *South Florida Sun-Sentinel,* "If you want brutal honesty, you've come to the right book with *Velvet Elvis.* It's a sensitive yet radical plea for simple Christian living, as stripped down as the alternative rock music Bell once played."

Taking His Message on the Road

On June 30, 2006, in Chicago, Bell began a speaking tour of the United States, with a theme of "Everything Is Spiritual." The tour was a great success, with tickets selling out everywhere. Besides helping to spread Bell's message, the tour also provided a big boost for a charity called WaterAid, which helps to improve and expand access to safe water supplies around the world. All profits from ticket sales to the "Everything Is Spiritual" tour were given to WaterAid.

In March 2007, Bell published his second book, with the attention-grabbing title *Sex God: Exploring the Endless Connections between Sexuality and Spirituality.* In this book, he discusses human urges and physical relationships and the ways they reflect the kind of love that exists between God and humankind. A reviewer for *Publishers Weekly* said that Bell "does a fine job using the Bible and real life to show that our physical relationships are really about spiritual relationships. This book joyfully ties, and then tightens, the knot between God and humankind." Bell made personal appearances on six college campuses to support *Sex God,* hosting sessions for questions and open conversation.

In addition to his books and tours, Bell began work on a series of inspirational videos known as NOOMA. Aimed at people ages 18 to 34, these short films combine music, narration, and visually striking locations—often in western Michigan—to promote spiritual responses to life situations and challenges. A small booklet is also included with the DVDs, which have such simple titles as *Trees, Rain,* and *Luggage.* Topics include love, death, faith, and forgiveness. The title NOOMA comes from the Greek word *pneuma,* which means spirit. Bell said the name reflected the "desire to be ancient while at the same time pushing forward." NOOMA videos increased Bell's following greatly, with approximately 1.2 million copies sold in more than 80 countries. In addition to being viewed by indi-

One of the inspirational NOOMA videos.

viduals, NOOMA films are also used by drug-recovery groups, professional sports teams, and other organizations, in locations as far away as Morocco and India.

In June 2007, Bell went on a short tour of the United Kingdom and Ireland, speaking on the topic "Calling All Peacemakers." In November 2007, he launched his "The Gods Aren't Angry" tour in the United States, traveling

17

to 22 cities to spread his message. Like his other tours, it was a sellout. His principal theme was that God only asks for faith and that requiring sacrifices to make God happy is a reflection of outdated ways of thought. All proceeds from "The Gods Aren't Angry" were given to Turame Microfinance, which helps to establish business ventures among underprivileged people in the country of Burundi. Religious speakers usually appear in churches or at religious festivals, but Bell broke with tradition and gave many of his talks in nightclubs or bars. He stated that he wanted to be booked into places where he might have a better chance of reaching "so many people [who have] been turned off by the packages Jesus has been presented in."

Bell and Don Golden, one of Bell's associates at Mars Hill, worked together to write *Jesus Wants to Save Christians: A Manifesto for the Church in Exile,* published in 2008. The book's message is that Christianity should be a means for helping people, not for justifying political ends, especially violence or war. Although it features the same brief sentences, eye-catching typography, and clever chapter titles as Bell's earlier books, *Jesus Wants to Save Christians* "offers more serious theological reflection and biblical commentary," said a reviewer for *Christianity Today.* "Bell and Golden draw readers into wrenching experiences such as Egyptian slavery, Babylonian captivity, and Roman tyranny."

Drops Like Stars: A Few Thoughts on Creativity and Suffering was published in 2009. It is a collection of brief anecdotes, which Bell uses to explore suffering, creativity, and the connection between them. Bell never attempts to answer a question that has troubled many people throughout the centuries: Why would a loving, all-powerful God allow creatures to suffer? Instead, he draws on his own experience as a pastor to comment on the good that frequently comes out of suffering. Examples could include the chance to make a new start, increased empathy for other people, or personal growth. Once again Bell toured to support the publication of *Drops Like Stars.*

Controversy over the Book *Love Wins*

With his book *Love Wins: A Book about Heaven, Hell, and the Fate of Every Person Who Ever Lived,* Bell expanded on the phrase "Love Wins," the message that Mars Hill Bible Church spreads on its bumper stickers. He sought to defuse the negative image of God as an angry, authoritarian figure who is intent on punishing those who don't measure up. He wanted to replace that image with one of a peaceful, loving, forgiving God. In his book, Bell looked at the many different ways that hell has been envisioned and described, yet, he did not state that any of them are correct. Instead, he expressed a hope that, in fact, the love of God is so great that no one can be outside it, and that in the end, all will be brought to heaven because of God's great love. He asserted that heaven is a real place, but expressed some doubts about hell.

This message was very controversial, especially to the Protestant evangelical tradition from which Bell came. For the most part, evangelical Christianity places utmost importance on the belief that the soul can only reach heaven through a belief in and acceptance of Jesus Christ as the son of God and the savior of humanity. Hell, in that tradition, is very real. Bell's suggestion that everyone might be saved and spend eternity in heaven, no matter how they lived their life or what they believed, was offensive to some Christians. They felt that it ignored or distorted Bible teachings, as well as minimizing the importance of Jesus. Some people felt that Bell had moved from an evangelical Christian stance to one of Universalism, a body of religious thought that suggests that many belief systems hold core truths and are valid. Some Christians feel this is a dangerous school of thought, because it dilutes the importance of the truths revealed in the Bible.

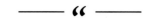

"Our founding pastor, Rob Bell, has decided to leave Mars Hill in order to devote his energy to sharing the message of God's love with a broader audience.... While we recognize that no one person defines a community, we acknowledge the impact of Rob's leadership, creativity, and biblical insights on our lives, and face a deep sadness at the loss of their presence in our community."

Bell had denied that his thought was Universalist in nature, however. He has said that he believes that Jesus is the key to salvation, and yet, he has also maintained that Jesus must be bigger than any religious differences found in the world. "I affirm the truth anywhere in any religious system, in any worldview," Bell has said. "If it's true, it belongs to God." He has said that he believes it is crucial to acknowledge that there are mysteries about the world and God, which humans are incapable of understanding completely. He is more interested in asking questions than in having all the answers. "I like to say that I practice militant mysticism," he explained. "I'm really absolutely sure of some things that I don't quite know."

In his sermons, Bell has expressed views that have attracted many followers, but some have proven controversial.

Despite the controversy over Bell's message, many Christians did accept and praise *Love Wins*. "Bell's writing can be choppy at times," Peter W. Marty wrote in *Christian Century*. "Seven consecutive incomplete sentences hardly make for grammatical coherence. But these deficiencies do not distract from the force of the larger argument. Bell has given theologically suspicious Christians new courage to bet their life on Jesus Christ." Richard Mouw, the president of Fuller Theological Seminary, wrote in his blog: "Rob Bell is calling us away from a stingy orthodoxy to a generous orthodoxy."

"Jesus is more compelling than ever," Bell has said. "More inviting, more true, more mysterious than ever. The problem isn't Jesus; the problem is what comes with Jesus." He preaches that instead of focusing on complicated belief systems with rigid rules, people should work to help other people in whatever ways they can. "We're rediscovering Christianity as an Eastern religion, as a way of life," he said. "We grew up in churches where people knew the nine verses why we don't speak in tongues, but had never experienced the overwhelming presence of God."

"Rob Bell is a central figure for his generation and for the way that evangelicals are likely to do church in the next 20 years," said Andy Crouch, an editor at *Christianity Today*. "He occupies a centrist place that is very appealing, committed to the basic evangelical doctrines but incredibly creative in his reinterpretive style."

"He's figured out how to convey basic Christian doctrine in a highly skeptical culture," said Quentin J. Schultze, a professor of communication at Calvin College in Grand Rapids. "He's very challenging in his sermons. There's no appeal for money. You get a sense of intellectual substance and depth of the faith."

In 2011, Bell surprised many when he announced that he was leaving his position at Mars Hill. In a statement, the church announced that "Our founding pastor, Rob Bell, has decided to leave Mars Hill in order to devote his energy to sharing the message of God's love with a broader audience.... While we recognize that no one person defines a community, we acknowledge the impact of Rob's leadership, creativity, and biblical insights on our lives, and face a deep sadness at the loss of their presence in our community." Bell revealed that he was working on writing a spiritual TV drama called "Stronger" that would be loosely based on his own life. The show would focus on Tom Stronger, a musician and teacher, and his spiritual journey as he works with other people. Music is expected to be a big part of the show. Bell and his family will be moving to Los Angeles, where he will also continue to write books and speak on tour.

As Bell faces new challenges, he is likely to keep looking for new ways to spread a positive message: That God loves the world, and people should try to be more Godlike in their love of each other. "For many people, there's a widespread, low-grade despair at the heart of everything," he noted. "If we can tilt things a few clicks in the hope direction, that would be beautiful."

HOME AND FAMILY

Bell and his wife Kristen have three children. Currently, they make their home in a renovated house in the inner city of Grand Rapids.

HOBBIES AND OTHER INTERESTS

Bell takes part in soccer games twice a week, goes to boxing lessons, and likes to water-ski, snowboard, and skateboard. He enjoys cooking and eating healthful food. He loves to read books and magazines on all subjects. "Economics, art, politics. I get on a subject and learn everything I can about it," he said.

Music is very important to him. In addition to playing with ___ ton bundle, from 1995 until 1997 Bell was part of a Christian punk rock band called Big Fil, which recorded two CDs: *Big Fil* and *Via de la Shekel.*

CREDITS

"NOOMA" video series, 2001-2009
Velvet Elvis: Repainting the Christian Faith, 2005
Sex God: Exploring the Endless Connections between Sexuality and Spirituality, 2007
Jesus Wants to Save Christians: A Manifesto for the Church in Exile, 2008 (with Don Golden)
Drops Like Stars: A Few Thoughts on Creativity and Suffering, 2009
Love Wins: A Book about Heaven, Hell, and the Fate of Every Person Who Ever Lived, 2011

HONORS AND AWARDS

100 Most Influential People in the World (*Time* magazine): 2011

FURTHER READING

Periodicals

Christian Century, May 17, 2011
Christianity Today, Mar. 24, 2009, pp.22-24; May 17, 2011, p.22
New York Times, July 8, 2006, p.A10; Mar. 5, 2011, p.A12
St. Petersburg Times, June 5, 2011, p.5P
USA Today, May 23, 2011, p.A11

Online Articles

www.bpnews.net
    (Baptist Press, "Rob Bell Book *Love Wins* Stirs Controversy, Denies Core Christian Beliefs," Mar. 15, 2011; "Hard-Hitting Rob Bell Interview Goes Viral," Mar. 16, 2011)
www.christianitytoday.com/ct/special/robbell.html
    (Christianity Today, "Rob Bell," multiple articles, various dates)

mlive.com
> (Mlive, "Profile: Mars Hill Bible Church Pastor Rob Bell," Mar. 23, 2008; "Profile: U.S. District Court Judge Robert Holmes Bell," Feb. 13, 2011; "Trendy Grand Rapids Pastor Leaving Church He Founded to Pursue 'Strategic Opportunities,'" Sep. 23, 2011)

topics.mlive.com/tag/Rob%20Bell/index.html
> (Mlive, "Rob Bell," multiple articles, various dates)

www.time.com
> (Time, "Pastor Rob Bell: What If Hell Doesn't Exist?," Apr. 14, 2011; "Rob Bell," Apr. 21, 2011)

www.usatoday.com
> (USA Today, "Megachurch Pastor Rob Bell Seeks Life Beyond the Pulpit," Sep. 23, 2011)

ADDRESS

Rob Bell
Author Mail, 11th Floor
HarperCollins Publishers
10 East 53rd Street
New York, NY 10022

WEB SITES

www.robbell.com
marshill.org

BIG TIME RUSH
Logan Henderson 1989-
James Maslow 1990-
Carlos Pena Jr. 1989-
Kendall Schmidt 1990-

American Pop Music Group, TV Actors, and
Stars of the Nickelodeon Series "Big Time Rush"

EARLY YEARS

Big Time Rush is a pop music group whose members also star
in a television series. The group includes four musicians/actors:
Logan Henderson, James Maslow, Carlos Pena Jr., and Kendall
Schmidt.

Logan Henderson

Logan Phillip Henderson was born on September 14, 1989, and raised in North Richland Hills, Texas, which is part of the Dallas-Fort Worth metropolitan area. He started singing at a young age and was surrounded by music in his home. "My family is pretty musical," he said. "Growing up, I'd listen to blues and old rock on the radio with my dad. I got a lot of my musical influences from older artists." Among the musicians that he admires are Aerosmith, the Beatles, B. B. King, Billie Holiday, Elvis Costello, and Prince. Henderson also became interested in acting and began attending an acting studio in the Dallas-Fort Worth area. Fellow Texans Demi Lovato and Selena Gomez were in some of his classes. Henderson became friends with both girls, and they have remained close as they have pursued their show-business careers.

"We got along like brothers from the start and have only grown closer since then," Maslow said. "In the show, as our characters, we have a very high energy and let problems like girls separate us, but in real life in the band we are all much more laid back."

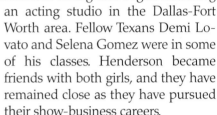

At age 16, Henderson landed his first notable role when he was cast for a small part in the TV series "Friday Night Lights," which was filmed in Texas. His next big break came when he took part in one of the auditions for "Big Time Rush" that were held all around the country, but it would be over 18 months before the producers made their final choices for the show. In the meantime, he made the decision to move to California to pursue his acting career, with the approval of his mom and dad. "I remember my parents saying, 'As long as you're doing something and giving it your all, we're going to back you up,'" Henderson said. He left home at age 18 and arrived in Los Angeles, joining the thousands of other young people in that city seeking a place in the entertainment industry.

James Maslow

James David Maslow was born in New York City on July 16, 1990. During his early childhood, his family lived in Florida and Chicago before settling in La Jolla, California, when he was six years old. That same year, his mother signed him up for the San Diego Children's Choir. "I didn't like it at first," he remembered, "but within two weeks I totally fell in love with it and then knew I'd be performing in some way all my life." Maslow learned

Big Time Rush on location in Santa Monica: (from left) Carlos Pena Jr., James Maslow, Logan Henderson, and Kendall Schmidt.

to sing and act by attending the San Diego School of Creative and Performing Arts and the Coronado School of the Arts, and he learned to play both guitar and piano. He is also a skilled athlete and was a member of the soccer, baseball, and basketball teams at his high school.

An experienced stage performer, Maslow appeared in *La Boheme* with the San Diego Opera and also in productions of *Les Miserables* and *Grease*. His first big break on TV was in a 2008 episode of the "iCarly" series, when he played Shane, a cute boy who sparks a fight between Carly and her friend Sam. Though his parents played an important role in his career, he prides himself on his independence and has lived on his own since age 17.

Carlos Pena Jr.

Born on August 15, 1989, Carlos Roberto Pena Jr. hails from a diverse Hispanic background. His mother is from the Dominican Republic, and his father is of Spanish and Venezuelan heritage. He spent his early youth in Columbia, Missouri, before moving to Weston, Florida. There, he joined a boy's choir, was trained in musical theater, and learned to play guitar and piano. His love of acting began at age 13, when he appeared in a school musical version of *Titanic* while a student at the American Heritage School in Plantation, Florida. At about the same time, he won a part in a Super Soaker water gun advertising campaign, and that work helped him focus his attention on a career in show business. "From [that point on,] I wanted TV, film, acting, singing, theatre ... anything," he said.

Around the time he was 15, Pena began to land guest roles on a number of different TV series, including "E. R.," "Judging Amy," and "Summerland." Another big break was winning a recurring part in "Ned's Declassified School Survival Guide" on the Nickelodeon cable network. The series was created by Scott Fellows—the man who would soon start work on "Big Time Rush"—and the role helped make Pena a familiar face to young viewers. In 2007, he got his first taste of what it might be like to be in a "boy band," when he was one of the 15 performers chosen to appear on the MTV reality show "Making Menudo." The program sought to create a new version of the popular 1980s Latino singing group Menudo, and Pena made it to the final nine contestants before being eliminated. He built a solid list of TV acting credits while in his teens and spent a lot of time in California working on programs. But he decided to complete his high school studies back home in Weston at the Sagemont School, graduating in 2008. He then set his sights on attending the Boston Conservatory, one of the country's elite schools for the performing arts. His plans to earn a degree there were interrupted after he became involved in the auditions for "Big Time Rush."

Kendall Schmidt

Kendall Francis Schmidt was born on November 2, 1990, in Wichita, Kansas, and was raised in the nearby town of Andover. He was the youngest of three sons in a family that became very involved in the entertainment industry. Both of his brothers, Kenneth and Kevin, became child actors, and his parents, Kent and Kathy Schmidt, supported their sons as they sought to establish themselves in the business. As a result, the family lived in New York City for a time and frequently traveled back and forth between Kansas and California. Wishing to follow in his older brothers' footsteps, Kendall began attending auditions and got his first acting job at age six, when he appeared in a cereal commercial along with Kenneth and Kevin.

The Schmidt family moved to the Los Angeles area when Kendall was ten years old, and they lived for five years at the Oakwood apartment complex, which is home to many aspiring actors. As a result, Kendall got to know many people who would go on to become stars. Actresses Kirsten Dunst and Christina Milian were his babysitters, and he was also acquainted with Hilary Duff. He soon began winning roles in such TV programs as "E. R.," "Mad TV," and "Frasier," and he was a recurring character on "General Hospital," "Gilmore Girls," "CSI: Miami," and other shows. He has also worked on films and was a double on the film *A. I.: Artificial Intelligence*, directed by Steven Spielberg. Schmidt's success, as well as that of his brothers, stemmed from assistance they got from their parents, and he has given a lot of credit to his mother and father. "I really couldn't have done anything if it wasn't for my parents being very supportive," he said in the *Boston Herald*. "It's not very often that parents drop everything and take their kids where they want to go to do what they want to do. I gotta give my dad a lot of props for holding strong."

FORMING THE BAND

Unlike most musical acts, Big Time Rush existed as a concept well before it had any actual members. The original idea for the band and TV program was hatched by Scott Fellows, who created "Ned's Declassified School Survival Guide" and has been a writer and producer on many Nickelodeon series. Because "Big Time Rush" is a TV show as well as a musi-

> *When asked who in the band is the biggest star, Schmidt responded that "it really depends on where we are, state by state. We did a promo tour across the U.S. and every state seems to like one of us more than the others. I would say that it evens out and it's pretty hard to say who is the most popular guy in the band!"*

cal ensemble, it was put together the same way that TV shows are created: the producers held auditions to find an actor to fill each role in the group. That process took a long time. Auditions began around 2007 and continued for more than a year and a half, with some 15,000 young performers trying to become part of Big Time Rush.

The slow pace was caused in part by the fact that the people chosen for the group had to be skilled both as actors and singers, had to have the "look" that the producers were seeking, and had to have good on-camera chemistry with one another. Henderson and Maslow had taken part in some of the first auditions for the show, so they faced many months of waiting before they got the good news that they had made the cut. According to one

Big Time Rush came together as a band in 2009, and their TV show debuted in November that year. From left: Kendall Schmidt, Carlos Pena Jr., Logan Henderson, and James Maslow.

source, Pena was initially not very interested in the program but finally decided to send in an audition tape and was offered his part a month later. Schmidt was the last of the four to be cast.

Once the lineup was set, Fellows shaped the characters in the show to create a good fit for the actors. "We didn't want four kids who looked alike," said Majorie Cohn, a Nickelodeon executive. "Each one brought some of their personality to the table, which in turn inspired (creator) Scott (Fellows)." In the process of building the show, Fellows decided to use the first name of each actor as the name of their TV character. Kendall Schmidt plays Kendall Knight, the leader of Big Time Rush. Logan Henderson portrays Logan Mitchell, the "brain" of the band, who helps the members find their way out of trouble. James Maslow has the part of James Diamond, the egotistical "pretty boy" of the ensemble. And Carlos Pena plays Carlos Garcia, the fun-loving jokester who is always ready to stick up for his friends.

CAREER HIGHLIGHTS

The plot of the "Big Time Rush" TV show concerns four hockey-playing friends from Minnesota who suddenly find themselves in Los Angeles, striving to become a successful boy band singing group. Their adventure begins when Kendall is accidentally discovered by a record producer during a nationwide casting call for singers. Not wishing to leave his friends behind, he talks the producer into allowing Logan, Carlos, and James to become part of the act. Soon, they are in California, where they work to establish themselves in the music industry.

In creating a show for young viewers that centers on pop music, the producers were carrying on a recent trend that had been established with the success of "Hannah Montana" as well as series such as "Jonas" and "Glee!" that debuted just months before the "Big Time Rush" premier. An important part of the marketing plan for such programs is to make the performers successful in two different media: as TV actors and as musical artists. In that way, the TV show helps promote the music, the music helps promote the show, and both—hopefully—make money.

The series was also influenced by several other factors. Fellows was inspired by the pop band the Monkees. The group was created in the late 1960s to star in its own TV series but also became a popular act in its own right, with numerous hit records. In addition, the decision to make Big Time Rush a boy band built on the success of similar groups, including N Sync and Backstreet Boys, both of which became popular in the 1990s. Of course, the importance of having four cute performers in the band to appeal to young female fans was lost on no one. As Henderson observed in an interview with *Seventeen*, "a lot of our show takes place in or around a pool, so there's not always a lot of clothes on us."

Big Time Success

After months of preparation and production, "Big Time Rush" debuted on Nickelodeon in November 2009 with a special two-hour preview episode and then began its regular schedule in January 2010. It was clear from the outset that the show was going to be a success. When the first January episode was broadcast, it became the highest rated premier for a live-action series in the history of Nickelodeon, drawing 6.8 million viewers, and it has averaged a healthy audience of 3 million per episode ever since.

The group's music proved popular as well. Big Time Rush began releasing singles for digital download shortly after the show went on the air: its first album, *BTR*, came out in October 2010 and went gold, meaning it sold more than 500,000 copies. A Christmas-themed extended play (EP) release, *Holiday Bundle*, followed in late November of that year.

Big Time Rush began working up a stage act for concert performances soon after being formed. Their live shows began in May 2010 but were limited at first to brief promotional appearances. Their later concerts included a series of special appearances at schools around the United States, with the locations being decided by contests in which the students sent in text messages to show their school spirit. In 2011, the band made appearances in Europe and then embarked on its first U.S. tour as a headline act, with the majority of the shows taking place at fairs around the country.

Truth or Fiction?

On the one hand, Big Time Rush is group of actors playing made-up characters on a TV show. On the other hand, the band puts out real recordings and plays real concerts. That combination can make it difficult for fans to figure out where make-believe ends and reality begins. In many ways, the two are mixed together, and the show's plot mirrors some of the real-life experiences of the actors. This is especially true of the scenes in which the members undertake "pop 101" studies to learn about the music industry. "The first episode is a caricature of what actually happened," said Maslow. "We went through boy band boot camp.... In real life it doesn't have the same over the top energy we have on the show but, that's actually our lives."

It would be a mistake, however, to think that the actors are exactly the same as the people they play on the show. "I'm actually completely opposite of my character," explained Pena, who plays the freewheeling Carlos Garcia. "He has fun and does whatever he wants … [but] I think that out of all four of us in real life, I'm the calmest." Maslow has made a similar point. "We're very different," the actor said, referring to his character. "James Diamond is really motivated by material objects and rewards, money and cars. I am motivated by the opportunity to do this, to perform, and to do it forever." Maslow also noted that "I don't usually care as much as [James Diamond] does about my hair or what I'm wearing."

One of the biggest questions about the blurring of real and imaginary elements concerns the band's music: are they really musicians or are they actors pretending to be musicians? Henderson addressed that issue by explaining that "we are actors making a show, but we are a real band in real life.… The music is all from us. Everything you hear is actually us."

The group does have help in creating its records. They draw on the expertise of a number of well-known producers and songwriters who have worked with such artists as Katy Perry, Kelly Clarkson, and Britney Spears. "All the producers we work with have been extremely cool," noted Schmidt. "I don't think we've come across anyone that hasn't let us have our input. We'll throw a harmony or something in there, and they'll love it so they put it in there." The members have also gotten involved in song-

The band's first album debuted in 2010 and went gold.

writing, contributing to the creation of the song "Oh Yeah." Moreover, several of the members have other outlets for their musical talent, including Schmidt, who is part of the electro-rock duo Heffron Drive.

Keeping It Friendly

On the TV show, the members of Big Time Rush play a group of good friends, which leads to the question of how close the performers are in real life. Since they hailed from different parts of the country, they did not know one another before becoming involved in Big Time Rush. Even though they were suddenly thrown together, there have been few problems. "We got along like brothers from the start and have only grown closer since then," Maslow said. "In the show, as our characters, we have a very high energy and let problems like girls separate us, but in real life in the band we are all much more laid back." The members of the group have admitted that they sometimes argue over small matters, largely as a result of having to spend so much time together, but are united by their desire to succeed. "We've been lucky enough to stay out of fights," said Henderson. "You learn to work stuff out. It's not only sunshine and rainbows. But we have one singular vision of what we want this to be."

Jealousy among musicians can also sink a band in short order. Thus far, the four members seem to receive roughly equal attention in the media, and each has their devoted fans, which has helped to keep things on an even keel. When asked who in the band is the biggest star, Schmidt responded that "it really depends on where we are, state by state. We did a promo tour across the U.S. and every state seems to like one of us more than the others. I would say that it evens out and it's pretty hard to say who is the most popular guy in the band!"

Building the Brand

In spring 2011, Big Time Rush had good news on two fronts. Nickelodeon ordered a third season of the program, which will begin airing in January 2012. In addition, the song "Boyfriend" climbed to No. 72 on the Billboard Hot 100 list, making it the band's biggest hit to date and the second time they had placed a song on that elite chart. The popularity of "Boyfriend" was helped along by a music video that included an appearance by hip-hop star Snoop Dogg. This unusual pairing came about, in part, because of one of the rapper's children. "He told us that his daughter was a big fan [of Big Time Rush] and that once he knew that, it was a done deal," explained Pena. "Working with Snoop was just as awesome as anyone might think. He met all of our expectations and more. He's just as cool and relaxed as he appears."

The band members are looking ahead to other projects in addition to the series. There is a possibility that they will star in a made-for-TV movie, and their second full-length album was released in 2011. The performers have also used their fame to help others. They have taken part in fundraising events for the T. J. Martell Foundation, which seeks cures for cancer, leukemia, and AIDS, and they also appeared in public service announcements for the Presidential Active Lifestyle Award program that promotes exercise.

As they focus on building the popularity of the group, the band members are finding that being pop stars can be exhausting. Between shooting the TV episodes, recording songs, appearing at concerts, and meeting various other commitments, they put in very long hours. "I feel like for us, it's become like a lifestyle," noted Pena. "There's so much going on. I sleep, eat,

Performing at the 2011 Nickelodeon Kids' Choice Awards.

drink, wake up, everything—Big Time Rush." They have also found that, as celebrities, the attention they now attract has forced them to change the way they live. "You give up a piece of stuff you normally would do," explained Henderson. "But that's part of the show. That's why we are entertainers, why we do what we do." And some parts of fame are more pleasant than others. As Maslow said, "It's not that bad of a thing to have thousands of girls chasing you.... Most guys dream of that." Taking the bad with the good, the band members seem to be intent on making the most of their opportunity and to have a great time doing so. "I think this is going to go on for as long as we have fun," said Maslow, "and as long as our fans enjoy it."

HOBBIES AND OTHER INTERESTS

All of the members of Big Time Rush live in the Los Angeles area, with the exception of Maslow, who continues to reside in nearby San Diego but is considering moving to LA. In their spare time, they enjoy a variety of athletic activities. Water sports are especially popular. Maslow and Schmidt are into surfing, Henderson enjoys wake boarding, and Pena is a scuba enthusiast and a certified rescue diver. In addition, Henderson, Maslow, and Schmidt take part in other outdoor activities such as hiking, mountain climbing, and rock climbing, and all are three are also avid skateboarders.

Pena studies Tae Kwan Do and, like his character, is into hockey, though he plays on roller blades rather than on ice skates.

CREDITS

TV

"Big Time Rush," 2010-

Recordings

BTR, 2010
Holiday Bundle, 2010
Elevate, 2011

FURTHER READING

Periodicals

Boston Herald, Dec. 4, 2010, p.21
New York Daily News, May 24, 2011
New York Times, May 16, 2010, p.ST9

Online Articles

www.billboard.com
  (Billboard, "Big Time Rush Brings Boy Bands Back," Oct. 13, 2010)
www.kidzworld.com
  (Kidzworld, "Big Time Rush Q&A," Apr. 12, 2011; "Carlos Pena Bio,"
  "Kendall Schmidt Bio," "Logan Henderson bio," "James Maslow Bio,"
  "Q&A with James Maslow from BTR," all no date)
www.mtv.com
  (MTV, "Big TimeRush, Full Biography," no date)
www.seventeen.com
  (Seventeen, "Meet the Cast of Big Time Rush," Nov. 23, 2009; "Big Time
  Rush Answers 17 Questions," no date)

ADDRESS

Big Time Rush
Nickelodeon
4401 Sunset Blvd.
Los Angeles, CA 90027

WEB SITE

www.nick.com/btr
www.btrband.com

Cheryl Burke 1984-

American Dancer, Choreographer, and
First Professional Dancer to Win Back-to-Back
"Dancing with the Stars" Championships

BIRTH

Stephanie Cheryl Burke was born on May 3, 1984, in Atherton, California. Her mother, Sherri Bautista Burke, was born in
the Philippines and worked as a nurse before opening her
own medical staffing agency. Her father, Stephen Burke, is an
attorney. They divorced before she was one year old, and her
mother remarried in 1993. Burke has an older stepsister and a
younger half-sister.

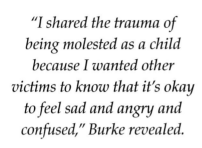

"I shared the trauma of being molested as a child because I wanted other victims to know that it's okay to feel sad and angry and confused," Burke revealed.

Burke switched the order of her first and middle names in a legal name change when she was in the first grade. She explained, "My parents thought it would be cute to give me names that were similar to theirs but unique enough to be my own…. But for a long time, they couldn't decide if I was more of a Stephanie or a Cheryl. Finally, when I was in first grade, I made the decision for them. 'From now on I want to be Cheryl. No more Stephanie,' I declared … and that's who I've been ever since."

YOUTH

Burke grew up in Atherton, California. She was an extremely shy child who did not begin speaking until she was much older than the typical age for this milestone. In an attempt to draw her out of her shell, her mother enrolled her in ballet lessons when she was four years old. She was soon dancing in performances throughout the San Francisco Bay area.

When Burke was five years old, she was molested by a neighborhood handyman that her mother and stepfather had hired to do some work at their home. The man had also molested other children in the neighborhood and was arrested once the children's parents discovered the abuse. When she was in kindergarten, Burke testified against the man at his court trial. Her statements helped to send him to prison.

Though the incident happened long ago, it is still difficult for Burke to talk about that time of her life. But she feels that it is important for her to tell her story, and she wrote about it in her autobiography *Dancing Lessons*. "I shared the trauma of being molested as a child because I wanted other victims to know that it's okay to feel sad and angry and confused," she revealed. "It's not easy, nor is healing an overnight process. But I want people to know that it is possible to move beyond those feelings and begin to win back your life from those memories. I'm living proof of that.

"I've thought a lot about that time in my life. I've been able to look back with a clearer understanding of what happened and how it affected many years of my life," Burke wrote. "I understand that many people have a very difficult time overcoming an experience like this. It's not easy. It takes time to heal. Although I am one of countless victims of that kind of crime, I made a concerted choice several years ago that I would not let it stop me from living my life—the life that I deserve. No longer would I allow this experience to control me." Burke also wrote about how she learned to deal with it. "I have learned that the molestation was not my fault. I did nothing wrong. As a child, it was normal for me to trust a grown-up," she explained. "Letting go of the resentment has been a gradual process, but it's very empowering. Every time I talk about it, it makes me stronger and more aware of what has made me who I am."

Discovering Ballroom Dance

Burke continued studying ballet throughout her childhood. She liked dancing, but as she grew up she began to realize that ballet might not be right for her. Her parents enjoyed ballroom dancing as a hobby, and she went to see a local dance competition with her mother. "I went to a competition and saw the costumes, heard the music, and loved that the dancers had partners," she recalled. That competition changed Burke's opinion of ballroom dancing. Before that, she had thought it was only for "old people" since her parents liked it. She began to take ballroom dance lessons when she was 12 years old.

By the time Burke was 13 years old, she was participating in as many ballroom dance competitions as she could. She travelled extensively and entered competitions all over the world. Once she became serious about ballroom dancing, her family all became more interested in the hobby. Her parents converted their home's living room into a small dance studio, and everyone spent most of their free time dancing there. Having a dance space at home also made it easier and more convenient for Burke to practice. Instead of driving back and forth to a dance studio in a nearby town, she could practice any time right in her own home.

"It's not easy, nor is healing an overnight process. But I want people to know that it is possible to move beyond those feelings and begin to win back your life from those memories. I'm living proof of that."

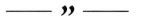

When she was a teenager, Burke and some of her friends decided they wanted to go to London, England, for the summer, to train and enter competitions. Her mother agreed to the plan, but said that she would have to raise part of the money to pay for the trip herself. Burke and her friends set to work immediately. They organized a dance camp for local kids and also danced for tips as street performers in San Francisco's Union Square. They raised enough money to pay for their air fare and to rent rooms in a small house in London.

EDUCATION

Although Burke spent a lot of time travelling to dance competitions while she was in high school, she was able to complete her studies on time. She graduated from Menlo-Atherton High School in 2002. After graduation, she wanted to focus on dancing full time, but her mother insisted that she go to college. Burke attended a local community college for one year, but she ended up leaving school to become a professional ballroom dancer.

CAREER HIGHLIGHTS

As a professional ballroom dancer, Burke spent her time in dance lessons, rehearsals, and competitions. She continued to travel all over the world to enter competitions and became known for her bubbly personality, creative choreography, and dazzling costumes. Though she competed in many forms of ballroom dance, her specialty was Latin dances. "For me, they are the most fun. They're energetic and the music and costumes are great."

In 2005, when she was 20 years old, Burke had her best year of competition ever. She won the San Francisco Open Latin Competition, the Ohio Star Ball Rising Star Competition, and the World Cup Professional Rising Star Latin Championship. She also won several other championships in the United States and the United Kingdom.

"Dancing With the Stars"

Burke's competition performances soon attracted the attention of talent scouts for a new reality competition show called "Dancing with the Stars." The new show was based on a British television show that paired star athletes, actors, musicians, and other public figures with professional dancers in a weekly competition. When she was 21 years old, Burke was invited to join the show's cast of professional dancers.

Burke's shy personality made her hesitant to consider the offer at first. "My immediate reaction was to turn them down because of my strong fear of cameras. But the more I thought about it, the more I figured, 'Why not? Give it a chance, at least, before you turn them down,'" she said. "I know it sounds unbelievable to say that I almost turned down the opportunity to star as a professional dancer on the hit reality dance show, but that's the truth." It was a decision that changed her life.

Dressed to dance.

Burke practicing with her season 2 partner, Drew Lachey. Lengthy rehearsals have been an important part of "Dancing with the Stars."

On "Dancing with the Stars," competition focuses on the ten basic styles of ballroom dance. In the Standards category, competitors perform the waltz, tango, Viennese waltz, slow fox-trot, and quick-step. The Latin category includes cha-cha, samba, rumba, paso doble, and jive. The show produces two seasons of competition each year. To prepare for each season, professional dancers and their celebrity partners begin training for four hours each day. As the competition goes on, training time increases to eight to ten hours each day, seven days a week. Burke explained that the grueling schedule is necessary for competitors to perform at their best. "Practice makes perfect. It takes a lot of time and energy to get it right and to go out there and perform. On the show you see celebrities who have no dance experience learn a dance in four or five days. They put in the time, and you see them exceed and improve every day. It all has to do with devotion and motivation."

Burke joined "Dancing with the Stars" for its second season, in 2006, and she quickly became a favorite of the TV viewing audience. She enjoyed choreographing the dances and teaching the moves to her partner, and she was also at home when performing the dances during the live competition shows. But Burke had trouble adjusting to one aspect of being a part of a hit TV show. "I was terrified of the cameras. The fame was new to me, and the whole idea of talking to the press was the scariest thing I could imagine, because I've always been a very shy and private person."

Burke credits her first celebrity partner, singer Drew Lachey, with helping her overcome some of her fears. "'Just focus on me,' Drew said. 'When you're talking to me, look at me and ignore the crew.' So I did," Burke wrote in her autobiography. "Thanks to Drew's constant efforts at drawing me out of my shell, I was able to let my personality start to emerge while the camera crews were there."

Though Burke wasn't always sure of herself in front of the camera, she was

———— " ————

"I do have curves—women are supposed to have curves. I always have, and I always will. I will never be the skeletal supermodel of magazines and runways and, frankly, I'm a lot healthier because of it. When the gossip magazines fixated on my weight, I eventually moved past being hurt just for myself.... I started to get angry for every 15-year-old girl who wants to try out for the cheerleading squad but is afraid because she worries she won't look good in the uniform."

———— " ————

completely confident on the dance floor. Burke won the "Dancing with the Stars" championship in her first two seasons on the show. In season two, she shared the honors with Drew Lachey. In season three, former NFL football player Emmitt Smith was her championship-winning partner.

This achievement made Burke the first professional dancer to win two championships and the first to win two in a row. These wins meant that she was starting to be recognized outside the small community of professional ballroom dancers. "It was a lot of fun but overwhelming at times, too, as I skyrocketed from being 'just a dancer' to 'that girl on "Dancing with the Stars.'" Burke began to get requests for more interviews and was a featured guest star on "The Suite Life of Zack and Cody."

Dealing with Criticism

Burke's success on "Dancing with the Stars" helped to raise the status of professional ballroom dancers and also attracted more interest in Burke herself. As she became more well-known, she often found herself being followed by paparazzi photographers. Stories about her began to appear in tabloid newspapers and gossip magazines. She had a hard time dealing with the unwanted attention, especially after an incident in 2008 when a tabloid published photos of her wearing a bikini. The photos set off a flurry of public commentary about her weight and her figure. People said that Burke was fat and began to speculate that she might even be pregnant.

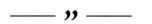

"I wanted to learn again and be a student, instead of always teaching.... I miss learning and sweating. I miss just going home and thinking about my dance and being inspired again, being coached. I love to teach, but I still feel like I have so much more to learn."

Burke took the comments hard. "It messed me up," she said. "I took the bloggers' criticism and negative comments personally, and I had a hard time maintaining a positive attitude." But she was also angry that people felt it was acceptable to make such comments. "No sane person thinks that a woman who is size four is overweight," she asserted. "I do have curves—women are supposed to have curves. I always have, and I always will. I will never be the skeletal supermodel of magazines and runways and, frankly, I'm a lot healthier because of it. When the gossip magazines fixated on my weight, I eventually moved past being hurt just for myself and became indignant for every woman out there who is perfectly normal yet fears that her body isn't beautiful. I started to get angry for every 15-year-old girl who wants to try out for the cheerleading squad but is afraid because she worries she won't look good in the uniform.

"I think a lot of young women struggle with taking compliments well. We find it easier to receive—and believe—criticism than a compliment. But that shouldn't be the case," Burke argued. "We should learn how to shake off negative comments that are intended to bruise our minds and instead allow ourselves to accept genuine compliments and constructive criticism. Compliments are a form of congratulations, celebrating something special about you," she said. "I just want everyone to know that, you know, you're beautiful in your own skin. You do not have to be anorexic or a size zero to feel great about yourself."

Branching Out

Burke's success on "Dancing with the Stars" has provided her with many opportunities to grow both personally and professionally. "The doors that have opened for me because of "Dancing with the Stars" and the perspective I have gained completely changed the way I view my life, my art, and my reason for dancing," she shared. "These opportunities have given me a new sense of strength and purpose that I believe can help to encourage other people to overcome the past, relate in new ways to the present, and reach for the future. It's made it possible to tell my story. All the hard things? You can move on from them. It's your choice."

Burke has toured the country with "Dancing with the Stars" and performed for sold-out crowds in many different cities. In 2006, her work on "Dancing with the Stars" was recognized with Emmy award nominations for Outstanding Choreography for Paso Doble and Outstanding Choreography for Freestyle. She received the Filipino/American Library's Role Model Award in 2007 and the Asian Excellence Viewer's Choice Award for Favorite TV Personality in 2008. Burke has also produced a dance exercise DVD and developed her own line of clothing for FitCouture.com. Demand was so high for her active wear that the retailer's web site crashed on the first day that the clothing was available for purchase.

At the request of her fans and with her mother's encouragement, Burke also achieved her lifelong dream of opening her own dance studio. The first Cheryl Burke Dance location opened in California in 2008. "I've wanted to open my own school since I was a little girl, and I got a lot of emails from fans asking when I would. They want to learn how to dance! And I really want to get young people into it, too, not just adults. It's fun, and kids can do it as a hobby or seriously," Burke explained. "I really want to promote physical fitness. And, you know, dancing is a way of life for me. And it's a great way to exercise."

Burke's "Dancing with the Stars" experience helped her to eventually overcome her fear of being on camera. In 2009, she became a correspondent reporter for the E! cable TV network and the show "Extra" and co-hosted the TV broadcast of the Citrus Bowl Parade in Orlando, Florida. In

*Burke performing with Rob Kardashian during the finals of season 13,
when they came in second.*

2010, her choreography was featured in the movie *Toy Story 3*. She and
"Dancing with the Stars" co-star Tony Dovolani choreographed the Latin
dance number performed by characters Buzz Lightyear and Cowgirl Jessie
in the movie. For this project, Burke and Dovolani performed the dance for
the film's design crew, who used their moves to create the animation for
Buzz and Jessie.

Burke achieved another of her lifelong dreams when she joined the *Forever Tango* touring stage show in 2010. *Forever Tango* showcases the Argentinian tango dance style and features performances by individual couples
and groups. The show has been in production off and on since 1994.
"Since I was a little girl, I've been a huge fan," she commented. "When
they were here in San Francisco performing, I remember my mom and
dad taking me to their performance and I fell in love with it right away. It's
part of how I got started into ballroom dancing, even though Argentine
tango and ballroom dancing are completely separate styles." To prepare
for *Forever Tango*, Burke spent three weeks studying the dance in Argenti-

na. "On ["Dancing with the Stars"] they added the Argentine tango a few seasons ago, and ever since I've been really interested in learning how to dance it properly. None of us ballroom dancers really know the actual technique of it. And I wanted to be re-inspired—I wanted to learn again and be a student, instead of always teaching.… I miss learning and sweating. I miss just going home and thinking about my dance and being inspired again, being coached. I love to teach, but I still feel like I have so much more to learn."

Throughout all of these new opportunities, Burke has continued competing on "Dancing with the Stars." Since partnering with Drew Lachey in season two and Emmitt Smith in season three, she has also danced with actor Ian Ziering; singer Wayne Newton; actor Cristián de la Fuente; track and field sprinter Maurice Greene; actor Gilles Marini; political leader Tom DeLay; football player Chad Ochocinco; basketball player Rick Fox; WWE wrestler Chris Jericho; and reality TV star Rob Kardashian.

After finding success in her dream field, Burke offers these words of advice. "You have to have a passion for what you do," she suggested. "If you don't, it won't work. Set goals in life. Follow your dreams and love what you do. Go for it 100 percent. Don't look back; keep looking forward."

HOME AND FAMILY
Burke has a home in the Hollywood Hills area of Los Angeles, California.

SELECTED CREDITS
"Dancing With the Stars," 2006- (TV show)
Dancing with the Stars: Latin Cardio Dance, 2008 (exercise DVD)
Forever Tango, 2010-2011 (stage show)
Dancing Lessons, 2011 (autobiography)

HONORS AND AWARDS
World Cup Professional Rising Star Latin Champion: 2005
San Francisco Open Latin Champion: 2005
Ohio Star Ball Rising Star Champion: 2005
Dancing with the Stars Championship: 2006 (season two)
Dancing with the Stars Championship: 2006 (season three)
Role Model Award (Filipino/American Library): 2007
Viewer's Choice Award (Asian Excellence Award): 2008, for Favorite TV Personality

FURTHER READING

Books

Burke, Cheryl. *Dancing Lessons*, 2011

Periodicals

Dance Magazine, Mar. 2008
Dance Spirit, Sep. 2008, p.140
Los Angeles Magazine, Oct. 2007, p.40
People, Oct. 20, 2008; Feb. 7, 2011
San Francisco Chronicle, Dec. 30, 2010, p.F1
USA Today, Mar. 26, 2007, p.D1; Oct. 16, 2007, p.D3

Online Articles

www.dancespirit.com
  (Dance Spirit, "Dancing with the Stars' Cheryl Burke Is Back," Sep. 1, 2006)
  (Dance Spirit, "A Q&A with Cheryl Burke from Dancing with the Stars," Sep. 21, 2008)

ADDRESS

Cheryl Burke
"Dancing with the Stars"
CBS Television City
7800 Beverly Blvd., Bungalow #1
Los Angeles, CA 90036

WEB SITE

www.strictlycheryl.com
abc.go.com/shows/dancing-with-the-stars/bios

Josh Hamilton 1981-

American Professional Baseball Player with the Texas
Rangers, American League MVP, and Batting
Champion in 2010

BIRTH

Joshua Holt Hamilton was born on May 21, 1981, in Raleigh,
North Carolina. His father, Tony Hamilton, worked as a super-
visor in factories that produced Wonder Bread baked goods
and Ditch Witch construction equipment. His mother, Linda
(Holt) Hamilton, worked for the North Carolina Department
of Transportation. Josh has an older brother, Jason.

YOUTH

Josh grew up as part of a family that loved sports, especially baseball. "Life in the Hamilton household revolved around family and baseball," he recalled. "You couldn't tell where one started and the other stopped—not on a dare." Both of his parents played in their youth, and they actually met for the first time at a softball game.

Josh showed exceptional ability as a baseball player from an early age. From the time he began playing Little League as a five-year-old, he frightened other players by hitting and throwing the ball much harder than they could handle. When Josh was seven, he could hit a ball 200 feet and clear the outfield fence. His talent was so remarkable that other parents began calling the commissioner of the league to express concern about the safety of their children. The commissioner responded by moving Josh up to the 12-and-under league, where he played with boys who were five years older than him—but much closer to his own skill level.

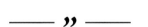

> *"Life in the Hamilton household revolved around family and baseball," he recalled. "You couldn't tell where one started and the other stopped— not on a dare."*

From the beginning, Josh's parents supported his interest in baseball by signing him up for leagues, coaching his teams, attending all his games, and teaching him the importance of discipline and hard work. Although his parents were a constant presence throughout his youth baseball career, Josh insisted that he never felt forced to play. "I was never pressured to play ball," he stated. "The perception of my parents as hard-driving stage parents was never accurate. I played because I loved to play, and because I was good at it."

EDUCATION

Hamilton attended Athens Drive High School in Raleigh. He made the varsity baseball team as a freshman, playing pitcher and center field. During his junior year in 1998, he posted an amazing .636 batting average with 12 home runs and 56 runs batted in (RBIs). As a senior in 1999, Hamilton batted .529 with 13 home runs and 35 RBIs, and he added 20 stolen bases. On the mound, he earned an 18-3 won-loss record for those two years, striking out 230 hitters in 143 innings. His achievements earned him the Gatorade High School Player of the Year Award for North Carolina in both his junior and senior seasons. He was also named the national High School Player of the Year by *Baseball America* for 1999.

By the end of his high school baseball career, Hamilton's talents had captured the attention of college coaches as well as Major League Baseball (MLB) scouts. As many as 60 professional scouts would attend his games—especially on the days when he pitched—armed with radar guns, stopwatches, and video cameras. They considered Hamilton to be a rare "five-tool prospect," meaning that he excelled in all five fundamental baseball skills that are typically evaluated by scouts: hitting for power, hitting for average, fielding, throwing, and speed. Everyone was certain that Hamilton would be selected in the 1999 MLB draft—the only question was whether he would be drafted as a pitcher or as an outfielder. "My preference was to be an outfielder, so I could play every day and do what I loved best—hit," he explained.

As draft day drew closer, several major-league teams evaluated Hamilton's off-the-field performance as well. They sent scouts to interview his teachers, friends, and teammates and even asked the young prospect to undergo psychological testing to predict how well he would handle stress. The MLB representatives were reassured to find Hamilton universally described as a polite, clean-cut, grounded kid from a good family. They learned that he was well-liked by teammates and even made a ritual of kissing his mother and grandmother for luck before every game. Shortly before graduating from Athens Drive High in the spring of 1999, Hamilton officially gave up his college baseball eligibility and made himself available for the MLB draft. "Faced with the possibility of being given the job of my dreams after high school graduation, choosing professional baseball over college was an easy decision," he noted.

CAREER HIGHLIGHTS

Turning Pro

The first overall pick in the 1999 draft was held by the Tampa Bay Devil Rays. Virtually all experts agreed that the club would use the choice to select either Hamilton or another prospect named Josh—a hard-throwing (and hot-headed) young pitcher from Texas named Josh Beckett. Partly on the basis of Hamilton's squeaky-clean image, the Devil Rays selected the big hitter from North Carolina instead. "Character may have been the determining factor," said Tampa Bay scout Mark McKnight. "You read so many bad things about pro athletes these days, but I don't think you ever will about Josh." Hamilton was determined to live up to the high expectations that came with being "one-one," or the first player selected in the first round of the draft. "I understood that being one-one came with a cer-

Tampa Bay general manager Chuck LaMar and draft pick Josh Hamilton hold up his new Devil Rays jersey after he was the first player taken in the draft in 1999.

tain responsibility that extended far beyond draft day," he acknowledged. "It was my responsibility to dictate whether the label would become a source of pride, or a burden."

Hamilton quickly reached an agreement with the Devil Rays on a lucrative contract that included a $4 million signing bonus. He launched his professional baseball career by playing for a Rookie League team based in Princeton, West Virginia, where he batted .347 with 10 home runs, 48 RBIs, and 17 steals. In 2000 he moved up to play for Tampa Bay's Class A affiliate, the Charleston River Dogs of the South Atlantic League. Hamilton continued his march toward the big leagues by batting .302 with 13 home runs, 61 RBIs, and 14 stolen bases in 96 games. During one game, he hit a towering home run that was measured at 549 feet—only 16 feet shorter than Hall of Fame great Mickey Mantle's all-time record. Although Hamilton's season was cut short by a knee injury, he was still named Most Valuable Player (MVP) of the league and Minor League Player of the Year. "That guy was a man among boys," recalled one of his Charleston teammates, Delvin James. "Some guys, you hear the hype and know it's just hype. But I'll tell you, you'll never see a more gifted, more skilled player than Josh Hamilton."

Team management's only concern about Hamilton involved his continued high level of dependence on his parents. He had used part of his signing bonus to pay off his parents' debts, which allowed them to retire from their jobs. Tony and Linda Hamilton decided to spend their newly acquired free time supporting their 18-year-old son. They followed Josh around the minor leagues, attended all of his games, offered him guidance, and even prepared his meals and did his laundry. Some people in the Tampa Bay organization worried that the constant presence of his parents would prevent Hamilton from maturing as a player and as a person. "The folks who ran the Devil Rays thought my parents' involvement was getting in the way of my becoming a man and learning to cope with life on my own. They also thought it was an obstacle to my bonding with my teammates," Hamilton explained. "I looked at it differently. They were here to make the transition easier, and we couldn't see how that could be seen as anything but positive."

> *"From the moment I tried cocaine, I became a different person," Hamilton related. "I became the coke-sniffing baseball player. I was a guy who was in violation of my contract, a guy who was willing to take a huge chance with his talent and his career, a guy who was willing to trade everything he'd achieved for temporary acceptance from a bunch of guys he didn't really know."*

Descending into Drug Addiction

Hamilton's life reached a turning point in March 2001, when he and his parents were involved in a serious car accident. A dump truck sped through a red light and hit their vehicle broadside, sending it spinning more than 100 feet. His parents suffered head and neck injuries and returned home to North Carolina to recover. Although Josh initially seemed unhurt, he soon began experiencing a stabbing pain in his lower back that affected his swing. He appeared in only 23 games for the Devil Rays' Class AA affiliate in Orlando during the 2001 season, and his batting average dropped to a dismal .180. Placed on the injured reserve list, Hamilton struggled with boredom and loneliness. "I won't downplay the importance of finding myself alone for the first time in my life. I've always struggled with free time," he admitted. "These events—the accident, my parents' leaving, my back hurting—created an environment where one bad decision could lead to many more."

Hamilton in the dugout during spring training in March 2003. He suited up for spring training but behaved erratically and ended up leaving the team. By this point he had started getting tattoos.

Hamilton took refuge from his feelings of uncertainty in an unusual place—a tattoo parlor. He started out by having his childhood nicknames ("Hambone" and "Hammer") tattooed on his biceps. These tattoos quickly led to more, and before long Hamilton was spending much of his free time hanging out at the tattoo parlor. He eventually ended up with close to 30 tattoos. "For me, the [tattoo] chair was an escape," he remembered. "I could sit there and escape from baseball and the people who wondered why I wasn't playing and the whispers that suggested I wasn't really injured and had lost my drive for the game. With my eyes closed and the ink taking shape under my skin, the world got a lot smaller. There were no expectations, nobody telling me how great I was or how great I could be."

Many people in the Devil Rays organization and in the media were shocked and dismayed to see the formerly straight-laced player covering his skin with designs and symbols. Some people wondered whether Hamilton was reacting to his sudden freedom from his parents' influence. "People say I was rebelling against my parents. That's not true. If my parents had been with me, none of this would have happened. I needed something, and I looked in the wrong place," he explained. "Clearly, the designs that kept springing up on my body, working from the top down, were an exterior sign of my interior confusion. In a sense, I became addicted to the feeling of getting tattoos—the first sign of my addictive personality."

While hanging out at the tattoo parlor, Hamilton was exposed to alcohol and drugs for the first time. The tattoo artists initially convinced the struggling young ballplayer to have a few drinks with them. Before long, Hamilton began snorting cocaine with his new "friends," and he quickly became addicted. "From the moment I tried cocaine, I became a different person," he related. "I became the coke-sniffing baseball player. I was a guy who was in violation of my contract, a guy who was willing to take a huge chance with his talent and his career, a guy who was willing to trade everything he'd achieved for temporary acceptance from a bunch of guys he didn't really know."

Deep in denial about his growing drug problem, Hamilton recovered from his back injury and returned to minor-league baseball in 2002. Playing in California for the Advanced Class A Bakersfield Blaze, he batted a solid .303 with 9 home runs and 44 RBIs before shoulder and elbow injuries ended his season prematurely on July 10. Although Hamilton did not know it at the time, that would be the last time he played in a professional baseball game for nearly four years. A short time later, he failed two consecutive drug tests and was suspended for 25 days for violating the MLB substance abuse policy. The Devil Rays sent him to the famous Betty Ford Clinic in California, named after its founder, former first lady Betty Ford, who courageously discussed her addiction publicly at a time when people hid such problems. A number of big-name athletes and movie stars have received treatment for addiction to drugs and alcohol at the Betty Ford Clinic. Hamilton insisted that he did not have a problem, though, and he left after a few days.

Hamilton's next three years deteriorated into a blur of failed drug tests, season-long suspensions from baseball, visits to various rehabilitation centers, brief recoveries, and repeated relapses. During this period he poured most of his $4 million signing bonus into drugs. In one six-week binge he threw away an estimated $100,000 on crack cocaine. His priorities changed so that baseball lost its meaning and drugs became all-important. "Drugs had taken over," he acknowledged. "They'd gone from a recreational mistake, something I stupidly thought I could control or ignore or deny, to a full-blown personal disaster. It was astonishing and perfectly natural how quickly drugs and the drug culture had taken up residence in my life."

Hitting Rock Bottom

In 2004, during one of his few extended periods of sobriety, Hamilton married Katie Chadwick. The couple had met through her father, Michael "Big Daddy" Chadwick, a former drug dealer and user who later became a successful home builder and youth minister. Hamilton had approached the elder Chadwick for help in beating his addiction, and he managed to stay sober for several months before he relapsed and began using drugs again.

Hamilton's addiction took a terrible toll on his wife. When Katie gave birth to their daughter in 2005, Hamilton left the house on an errand to pick up supplies for the newborn, ended up buying drugs instead, and did not return home for four days. On one occasion he even sold her wedding ring to buy drugs. Finally, after Hamilton flew into a violent rage while under the influence of drugs, his wife kicked him out of the house and took out a restraining order against him. "I'd been in rehab five or six times—on my way to eight—and failed to get clean. I was a bad husband and a bad father, and I had no relationship with God. Baseball wasn't even on my mind," he recalled. "Drugs had destroyed my body and my mind and my spirit. I could no longer experience happiness or surprise. I couldn't remember the last time I felt spontaneous joy. Why was I even alive?"

Hamilton finally hit rock bottom in October 2005. He awoke from a crack-cocaine binge in a dingy trailer surrounded by strangers and realized that he would not live much longer if he did not beat his addiction. "I prayed to be spared another day of guilt and depression and addiction," he remembered. "I couldn't continue living the life of a crack addict, and I couldn't stop, either. It was a horrible downward spiral that I had to pull out of, or die." Having alienated his wife and parents, Hamilton went to the only safe place he could think of—the home of his maternal grandmother, Mary Holt. When he showed up on her doorstep, he was dirty and unshaven, his nose was bleeding, he was coughing up a sticky black substance, and he had dropped 50 pounds from his once-muscular 230-pound frame. Nevertheless, his grandmother took him in, cleaned him up, fed him, and supported him as he started on the long road to recovery.

An important factor in Hamilton's recovery from drug addiction was reconnecting with his Christian faith. He turned his problems over to God, began attending church regularly, and devoted countless hours to Bible study. "I had been sober only a short time, but this time felt different," he explained. "When I surrendered to God, He took care of the rest. I had a peacefulness inside me, a calm that I hadn't felt since I started using." When he had remained clean for several months, Hamilton was able to reconcile with his wife and family. Then he began working himself back into playing shape at The Winning Inning, a baseball training academy that makes extensive use of Christian teachings.

An important factor in Hamilton's recovery from drug addiction was reconnecting with his Christian faith. "I had been sober only a short time, but this time felt different," he explained. "When I surrendered to God, He took care of the rest. I had a peacefulness inside me, a calm that I hadn't felt since I started using."

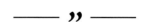

Making a Comeback

By the spring of 2006, Hamilton felt secure enough in his recovery—and confident enough in his physical skills—to seek a return to professional baseball. He sent a heartfelt letter of apology to Devil Rays management and MLB officials, along with a formal request for early reinstatement. He also sent along glowing testimonials from friends, relatives, religious leaders, drug counselors, and doctors to support his claims that he had finally beaten his drug addiction. In June 2006 Hamilton received news that he would be reinstated by MLB and allowed to participate in spring training. He returned to professional baseball that summer by playing 15 games for the Hudson Valley Renegades in a short-season Class A league.

In December 2006 Hamilton received more good news. The Cincinnati Reds had selected him in the Rule 5 draft, an annual event that is intended

Playing for the Cincinnati Reds in 2007, Hamilton slides across the plate to score, beating the tag by Philadelphia Phillies catcher Carlos Ruiz.

to prevent teams from hoarding major-league caliber players in their minor-league farm systems. Any young player that is not listed on a team's extended, 40-man roster can be picked up by another team for a small fee—as long as the acquiring team agrees to keep that player on its regular, 25-man roster for a full season. In effect, this development gave Hamilton a great shot at playing for the Reds in the big leagues during the 2007 season. "This was the kind of news I was afraid to pray for. This was sent directly from heaven, a phenomenal opportunity," he stated. "Number-one draft pick or not, I was a 25-year-old man with a history of serious drug problems and less than a hundred at-bats above Class A. In the past four years, I had played a total of 15 games, all at low-level Class A. And now I was being given the opportunity to make a major-league 25-man roster."

Hamilton rewarded the Reds' faith in him from the very beginning, posting an impressive .403 batting average in spring training. He made his long-awaited major-league debut on April 2, 2007, when he came in as a pinch hitter and hit a line drive that was caught for an out. A week later, on April 10, Hamilton made his first career start in a game against the Arizona Diamondbacks and tallied his first career hit, a two-run homer off pitcher Edgar Gonzalez. Hamilton finished his rookie season with a .292 batting average, 19 home runs, and 47 RBIs in 90 games.

Throughout the 2007 season, Hamilton stayed clean and sober with the help of an extensive support system. He kept in constant touch with a group of "accountability partners" that included his wife, his father-in-law, his grandmother, Raleigh pastor Jimmy Carroll, televangelist James Robison, and Christian sports agent Mike Moye. "It is very important to my recovery and my walk with Christ that I have people like that around me," he noted. "They always call or text at the right time."

Hamilton's closest supporter was Johnny Narron, a former MLB first baseman who had been his youth basketball coach in Raleigh. Officially hired as an assistant batting coach for the Reds, Narron became Hamilton's mentor, confidant, chaperone, and friend. He kept track of Hamilton's whereabouts at all times and ensured that the recovering addict never carried credit cards or more than $20 cash, never went out alone at night, and rarely socialized with teammates after games. As a final precaution, the team required Hamilton to submit to a drug test every three days. "It reassures the people who made the decision to let me back in the game that things are good," he explained.

Joining the Texas Rangers

Following his successful rookie season, Hamilton was traded to the Texas Rangers in December 2007 for pitchers Edinson Volquez and Danny Herrera. The Rangers scouted Hamilton extensively and consulted with experts about drug addiction and recovery before making the deal. Hamilton made an immediate impact on his new team. He earned a position as the Rangers' starting center fielder by hitting an incredible .556 with 13 RBIs in 14 games during spring training. His impressive performance continued during the early regular season, when he became the first American League (AL) player to be named Player of the Month for two consecutive months.

While Rangers' fans recognized Hamilton's talent from the beginning, he only came to national attention at mid-season, when his statistics earned him a spot in the 2008 MLB All-Star Game. His remarkable comeback story attracted a great deal of media attention and fan interest, and people across the country enjoyed watching him rise above his troubled past to finally reach his potential. Invited to compete in the annual Home Run Derby as part of the All-Star festivities, Hamilton hit a record 28 home runs in the first round, including 13 in a row and 3 blasts longer than 500 feet. Although he finished with a total of 35 home runs, he lost in the final round of competition to slugger Justin Morneau of the Minnesota Twins.

Hamilton's bat cooled off a bit during the second half of the season, but he still finished with an impressive .304 average, adding 32 home runs and an AL-leading 130 RBIs. His strong performance helped the Rangers finish second in the AL West Division with a 79-83 record. At the end of the season Hamilton published a book about his life experiences, entitled *Beyond Belief,* co-authored by sportswriter Tim Keown.

In 2009 Hamilton endured several injuries that had a negative impact on his offensive numbers. He still managed to hit .268 with 10 home runs and 54 RBIs in 89 games, and he was selected to the All-Star team for the second time. The Rangers ended the season with an 87-75 record, which once again resulted in a second-place finish in the division. The most disheartening part of the season for Hamilton occurred in August, when the media revealed that he had relapsed and used alcohol several months earlier. Photographs appeared on the Internet that showed the Rangers star clearly intoxicated and behaving inappropriately with women in a bar. Hamilton admitted that he had made a mistake and said that he had already apologized to his wife, his teammates, and Rangers management. "You have to look at the positives," said Texas general manager Jon Daniels. "It was a reminder to Josh that he can't sneak off, that this can't happen privately. It made his system for dealing with it that much stronger."

Earning MVP Honors

Hamilton bounced back in 2010 to have one of the best offensive years in Rangers history. He was named Player of the Month for June after batting .454 with 9 home runs and a franchise record 49 hits, and he was selected to the All-Star team for the third consecutive season. Late in the season Hamilton collided with an outfield fence while trying to run down a fly ball. The collision resulted in broken ribs that forced him to miss 25 of the last 30 games of the season. Nonetheless, Hamilton still led the majors with a .359 batting average. He also added 32 home runs and 100 RBIs, and he led the majors in slugging percentage (a measure of power hitting that is calculated by dividing total bases by at-bats) with .633. The Baseball Writers Association recognized his stellar season by naming him Most Valuable Player in the American League, and he also received MLB Player of the Year honors from the *Sporting News* and *Baseball Digest.*

Hamilton's contributions helped the Rangers win the AL West Division with a 90-72 record and make the playoffs for the first time since 1999. "We have more fun than any team in baseball, and I think it's evident in

Hamilton making a diving catch during the 2010 World Series.

the way we play," he declared. "We never give up until the last out is made. We always feel like we have a chance to win the game."

In the first round of the AL playoffs, Texas defeated Hamilton's former team, Tampa Bay, in 5 games. Still recovering from his rib injury, Hamilton hit a disappointing .143 with 2 hits in 14 at-bats during the series. He came back strong in the American League Championship Series (ALCS), when the Rangers defeated the defending champion New York Yankees in 6 games to claim the first pennant in franchise history. Hamilton was named ALCS Most Valuable Player for his performance, which included 4 home runs, 7 RBIs, and an ALCS-record 5 intentional walks. Unfortunately, the Rangers lost the 2010 World Series to the San Francisco Giants in 5 games. Hamilton managed only 2 hits (including a home run) in 20 at-bats against the Giants.

Facing Tragedy and Disappointment

Prior to the start of the 2011 season, Hamilton signed a two-year, $24 million contract extension with the Rangers. Although he was pleased with the deal, the year proved to be a difficult one for him. In April he broke his upper right arm while sliding headfirst into home plate, putting him out of action for more than a month. In July Hamilton was involved in a tragic accident. He casually tossed a foul ball into the stands, as players routinely do. A fan leaned out to try to catch it for his young son and fell to his death from the upper deck. Hamilton recognized that what happened was not his fault, but he felt terrible about it nonetheless. "It was a traumatic event. It's going to be around for a while," he acknowledged. "Just a random act of kindness turned tragic. It just lets you know how quickly life can change, just in the blink of an eye."

> "My story is bigger than me. Every time I go to the ballpark, I talk to people who are either battling addictions themselves or trying to help someone else who is. They want to confide in me, to share, to see if something I experienced can help them succeed as well…. They know where I've been. They look to me because I'm proof that hope is never lost. They remind me that this isn't really about baseball."

The Rangers moved past the tragedy to have a tremendous season, defending their AL West Division title with a franchise-best 96-66 record. Hamilton batted .298 with 25 home runs during the regular season and was voted to the All-Star Team for the fourth straight year. Texas then marched through the first two rounds of the playoffs, defeating Tampa Bay 3-1 in the divisional series and besting the Detroit Tigers 4-2 in the ALCS, to make a second consecutive trip to the World Series.

This time, Hamilton and his teammates faced the St. Louis Cardinals. After trading victories with their rivals in the first four games, the Rangers managed to take a 3-2 lead and seemed poised to win the first world championship in franchise history. In the potentially deciding Game 6, Texas came within one strike of victory on two different occasions. Instead, the Rangers suffered a heartbreaking 10-9 defeat in an 11-inning thriller. They could not overcome their disappointment in Game 7, and St. Louis won the clincher by a score of 6-2 to claim the World Series title.

Despite a painful sports hernia that limited his postseason performance, Hamilton managed to bat .271 during the playoffs, with 1 home run and 13 RBIs. "I've been hurt the last two years in the playoffs," he said afterward. "I could either be really resentful and mad, and grow apart from

*Hamilton hitting a two-run home run off a pitch by the Cardinals'
Jason Motte during the 2011 World Series.*

[God], or I could be satisfied that He got me through it again and grow closer to Him. I'm not mad, I'm not upset. I did what I could do."

Providing a Positive Example

Hamilton remains dedicated to serving God by providing a positive example and a message of hope for others who are fighting addictions. "My mission is to be the ray of hope, the guy who stands out there on that beautiful field and owns up to his mistakes and lets people know it's never completely hopeless, no matter how bad it seems at the time. I have a platform and a message, and now I go to bed at night, sober and happy, praying I can be a good messenger," he explained. "My story is bigger than me. Every time I go to the ballpark, I talk to people who are either battling addictions themselves or trying to help someone else who is. They want to confide in me, to share, to see if something I experienced can help them succeed as well.... They know where I've been. They look to me because I'm proof that hope is never lost. They remind me that this isn't really about baseball."

Hamilton feels pleased that he is able to inspire others with his story. He believes that his struggles have made him a better person, given him a sense of purpose, and allowed him to make a difference in people's lives. "This may sound crazy, but I wouldn't change a thing about my path to the big leagues," he noted. "If I hadn't gone through all the hard times, this whole story would be just about baseball. If I'd made the big leagues at 21 and made my first All-Star team at 23 and done all the things expected of me, I would be a big-time baseball player, and that's it." Hamilton frequently expresses gratitude that he was able to turn his life around and return to professional baseball. "I just feel so blessed that God allowed me to keep my skills, allowed me to not be brain-dead or dead period or in jail, that He allowed me the grace to be able to come back and be able to share my story and be able to play the game," he stated.

MARRIAGE AND FAMILY

Hamilton married Katie Chadwick in November 2004. Although he and his wife went to the same high school, they did not really know each other until Hamilton approached her father for help in conquering his drug addiction. Katie had a daughter, Julia (born in 2001), from a previous relationship when they got married. They also have two daughters together, Sierra (2005) and Michaela (2008).

HOBBIES AND OTHER INTERESTS

Hamilton and his wife formed a charitable foundation called Triple Play Ministries "to spread the word of God and assist others in overcoming obstacles and challenges." The organization is involved in sports ministry, community outreach, and mission projects. Hamilton enjoys using his talents in baseball and his life experiences as a platform to share his faith and spread his message of hope.

HONORS AND AWARDS

Gatorade High School Player of the Year (North Carolina): 1998, 1999
High School Player of the Year (*Baseball America*): 1999
Minor League Player of the Year (*USA Today*): 2000
Silver Slugger Award: 2008
American League All-Star Team: 2008, 2009, 2010, 2011
American League Most Valuable Player (Baseball Writers Association): 2010
American League Championship Series (ALCS) Most Valuable Player: 2010
Major League Baseball Player of the Year (*Sporting News* and *Baseball Digest*): 2010

FURTHER READING

Books

Hamilton, Josh, with Tim Keown. *Beyond Belief: Finding the Strength to Come Back,* 2008

Periodicals

Baseball Digest, Sep./Oct. 2010, p.14; Jan./Feb. 2011, p.24
Current Biography Yearbook, 2011
ESPN The Magazine, June 24, 2004; July 16, 2007
Sporting News, Sep. 27, 2010, p.34
Sports Illustrated, Apr. 12, 2004, p.56; June 2, 2008, p.30

Online Articles

sports.espn.go.com
    (ESPN, "Hell and Back" and "I'm Proof That Hope Is Never Lost," July 15, 2008)
www.dallasnews.com
    (Dallas News, "Josh Hamilton Finds Strength after Misstep in Recovery from Addiction," Oct. 4, 2010)

ADDRESS

Josh Hamilton
Texas Rangers Baseball Club
PO Box 90111
Arlington, TX 76004-3111

WEB SITES

tripleplayministries.com
texas.rangers.mlb.com

Bruno Mars 1985-

American Singer, Songwriter, Music Producer, and Creator of the Hit Songs "Just the Way You Are," "Grenade," "Nothin' on You," "Forget You," and "Billionaire"

BIRTH

Bruno Mars was born Peter Gene Hernandez Jr. on October 8, 1985, in Honolulu, Hawaii. His mother, Bernadette Hernandez, a former professional singer and hula dancer, is Filipino (from the Philippines). His father, Pete Hernandez, a Latin drummer and singer, is Puerto Rican. Mars has four sisters and one brother. His father gave him the nickname "Bruno" when he was two years old because he was chubby like the professional wrestler Bruno Sammartino. Bruno adopted the surname "Mars" later, when people called his stage performances "out of this world."

YOUTH

Mars grew up in a family that loved music. His father was a well-known musician in the Waikiki Beach area of Honolulu. When Mars was very young, his parents, uncles, and other family members frequently performed on stage in a popular musical show produced by his father. Mars decided early on that he wanted to be part of the show. "Yeah, from a very young age I remember watching the show and being completely fascinated. You know, my uncle would be up there playing guitar, my dad would be up there conducting the whole show, my mom would be singing out.... And I'd be like 'I wanna go up there too!'"

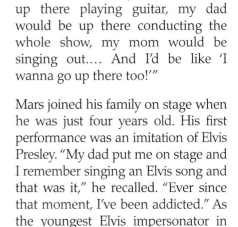

> When Mars was very young, his family frequently performed on stage in a popular musical show. "From a very young age I remember watching the show and being completely fascinated. You know, my uncle would be up there playing guitar, my dad would be up there conducting the whole show, my mom would be singing out.... And I'd be like 'I wanna go up there too!'"

Mars joined his family on stage when he was just four years old. His first performance was an imitation of Elvis Presley. "My dad put me on stage and I remember singing an Elvis song and that was it," he recalled. "Ever since that moment, I've been addicted." As the youngest Elvis impersonator in Hawaii, Mars quickly became a popular feature in his father's stage shows. His performances attracted so much attention that at one point, his parents were summoned to a family court hearing where they had to prove that young Mars was not being forced to perform. The judge was satisfied that he was not being forced on stage when the little boy got up on a table in the courtroom to sing and dance. Mars's early fame led to a cameo appearance as Little Elvis in the 1992 comedy movie *Honeymoon in Vegas*.

The family stage show ended with the divorce of his parents when Mars was ten years old. After that, he and his brother lived with their father while his sisters lived with their mother.

EDUCATION

Mars attended President Theodore Roosevelt High School in Honolulu, where his favorite classes and activities were in the performing arts. Mars was involved in school musicals and directed one of the school's stage plays. He choreographed performances at school pep rallies and also founded a doo-wop singing group called the Schoolboys. (Doo-wop is a rhythm and blues style of music that was popular in the 1950s. It typically involves several voices singing in close harmony, using words or nonsense syllables that fit the desired rhythm.)

Though the family musical act had been disbanded, Mars continued performing on his own during his teen years. He was featured in a Waikiki Beach musical revue as a Michael Jackson impersonator. In

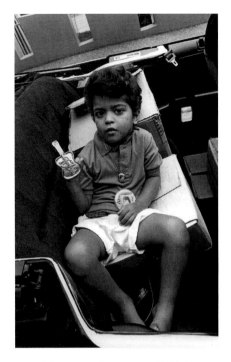

Mars as a four-year-old Elvis impersonator in 1990 in Memphis, Tennessee.

other stage shows, he performed the music of Motown recording stars like the Temptations and the Isley Brothers. When he was 16 years old, Mars was the opening act for a tourist entertainment show called "The Magic of Polynesia," a reference to the large group of islands located in the central and southern Pacific Ocean.

During these years, Mars developed a love of many different styles of music, including Motown, hip-hop, rhythm and blues, reggae, and rock. He also learned to play the guitar and drums. "Hawaii is basically in the middle of the world," he suggested, "so you're exposed to every type of music over there." During high school, music was such an important part of his life that he rarely went anywhere without his guitar or his ukulele. Mars graduated from Theodore Roosevelt High School in 2003.

CAREER HIGHLIGHTS

After high school Mars moved from Hawaii to Los Angeles to live with his brother. Only 17 years old, he began singing in small bars and night clubs.

Mars working on a song.

Though he often performed for very small audiences of only a few people, he was able to establish a reputation as a talented singer and musician. In 2004, Mars signed a recording contract with Motown records. At that time, he did not have a clear idea of the kind of record he wanted to make. He received little support from the record label, and after less than a year his contract was cancelled. He later said of this early disappointment, "My heart dropped out. It's not like the movies, where you get signed and you think hit songs are going to come to you and you tour the world. You've got to walk in there knowing exactly who you are."

Becoming a Songwriter

After being released from his contract with Motown, Mars realized that he needed to figure out on his own what kind of music he wanted to create. But meanwhile, he also needed a way to earn a living. Creating music was the only thing he knew how to do. In 2004, Mars stopped trying to make his own record and began to write songs for other more established artists to perform. He formed a songwriting and music production company called the Smeezingtons with two of his friends. "You know, because we were so broke back then I was like, 'I'm gonna forget the artist thing for the moment. We need to eat! So for now let's just concentrate on writing and producing and selling our tracks,'" he remarked. "It was either that or I was going back to Hawaii. After we sold the first track, it opened our eyes. We put the artist stuff on the back burner and took some of the pressure off ourselves."

With the Smeezingtons, Mars wrote many songs that went on to become hits performed by other artists. Some of the hit songs that he wrote during this time are "Long Distance" (recorded by R&B singer Brandy in 2008), "Right Round" (recorded by rapper Flo Rida in 2009), and "Wavin' Flag" (performed by rapper K'Naan in 2009). "Wavin' Flag" became an international hit when it was used as the theme song for the 2010 FIFA World Cup soccer tournament. Because of the amount of time that is usually required to create musical recordings, Mars actually wrote and sold these songs several years before the finished versions were released by the other performers. By 2006, he had become a well-known songwriter.

While he was writing songs for others, Mars never completely abandoned his dream of making his own record. He created sample recordings known as demos for each of the songs he wrote with the Smeezingtons. The main purpose of these demos was to sell the song to another artist, but Mars also thought that the demos might help him get his own recording contract. "We were just keeping our fingers crossed and hoping that somewhere along the way the [record company] executives were gonna listen to the guy singing on the demo of these songs—ME!—and be like 'This guy is good! Let's sign him!'" Mars admitted. "Which is exactly what happened when the label heard 'Nothin' on You.'" ("Nothin' on You" was later recorded and released by rapper B.o.B.) In 2006, Mars signed his own recording contract with Atlantic Records Elektra. "And that, in a nutshell, is the story of me becoming the solo artist you see today."

"You know, because we were so broke back then I was like, 'I'm gonna forget the artist thing for the moment. We need to eat! So for now let's just concentrate on writing and producing and selling our tracks,'" Mars remarked. "It was either that or I was going back to Hawaii. After we sold the first track, it opened our eyes. We put the artist stuff on the back burner and took some of the pressure off ourselves."

Breakout Success

Beginning in 2009, Mars enjoyed a string of successes. His breakout moment came when B.o.B. released "Nothin' on You," a track that showcased a unique mix of R&B and rap. B.o.B. performed the rap and Mars was the featured singer on the track. This was the first time that Mars was exposed to a large listening audience. "Nothin' on You" became an instant hit and was nominated for a host of music awards. These included the 2010 Soul Train Music Award for Song of the Year; two 2010 BET Awards, for Best Collaboration and Video of the Year; and three 2010 BET Hip Hop Awards, for Best Hip Hop Video, Perfect Combo Award, and People's Champ Award. The song also was nominated for awards at the 2010 MTV Video Music Awards, the 2010 Teen Choice Awards, the 2011 Grammy Awards, and the 2011 *Billboard* Music Awards.

The success of "Nothin' on You" was followed by the 2010 release of Travie McCoy's hip-hop/reggae single "Billionaire." Mars wrote "Billionaire" during the time when he was building his career as a songwriter and still struggling to make ends meet. "I was tired of spending half my day worrying about what I can and can't spend on whatever," he recalled. "I would have to worry about, you know, 'I can't afford to get breakfast, so I'll wait until lunchtime to eat.' If I was a billionaire, none of that would matter. I'd be eating diamond cereal." "Billionaire" sold two million singles in the first two months after it was released. Mars once again appeared as the featured singer on the track.

In 2010, Mars had another mega-hit with singer Cee-Lo Green's recording of "Forget You," a Grammy award-winning song that was co-written and co-produced by Mars, who also sang on the track. "Forget You" became a global smash hit that topped the *Billboard* music charts, sold almost four million downloads, and set off a viral video phenomenon. The song became a relationship break-up anthem that *Billboard* magazine called "a true cultural moment." It was nominated for three Grammy Awards in 2011, including Record of the Year and Song of the Year. "Forget You" won the 2011 Grammy Award for Best Urban/Alternative Performance.

By this time, Mars was attracting a lot of attention from the music industry, the media, and music fans. His string of hit records and his performances at the 2010 MTV Video Music Awards and the 2011 Grammy Awards presentation galas had audiences clamoring for more. In 2010, Mars released a four-song EP (extended play) recording called *It's Better That You Don't Understand*. This was his first release as a solo artist. The title refers to his reluctance to talk about the meaning or message that might be found in his music. When asked if his song lyrics are based on his own life experiences, Mars often replies, "It's better if you don't understand, just listen and have a good time."

Mars's first full-length CD including the hit song "Just the Way You Are,"
"Grenade, and "The Lazy Song."

Doo-Wops & Hooligans

Mars's EP was closely followed by the 2010 release of *Doo-Wops & Hooligans*, his debut full-length album. Though he dislikes talking about his songs or the lyrics he writes, he has explained the significance of the record's title. "'Doo-wop' is a very special word for me, because I grew up listening to my dad who, as a Fifties rock & roll head, loved doo-wop music. Plus doo-wop, again, is very simple! You know, I could get a guitar, play you just four chords, and sing a thousand doo-wop songs. Because they come from a time back in the day when there were no tricks. You just needed a beautiful melody, you needed a beautiful voice, and you needed to connect. And because to me, 'Just the Way You Are' just feels like it fits into that vibe, that's where the 'doo-wop' side of the title comes in. But, while the 'doo-wop' part is for the women, you also have to remember that I'm a young kid who likes partying and who gets up to some riff-raff sometimes. Which is in turn represented by the 'hooligans' side. So the title basically reflects that you get to hear the two sides of me on this one album."

"'Doo-wop' is a very special word for me, because I grew up listening to my dad who, as a Fifties rock & roll head, loved doo-wop music. Plus doo-wop, again, is very simple! You know, I could get a guitar, play you just four chords, and sing a thousand doo-wop songs. Because they come from a time back in the day when there were no tricks. You just needed a beautiful melody, you needed a beautiful voice, and you needed to connect."

"Just the Way You Are" was the first single and video released from *Doo-Wops & Hooligans*. The track received heavy radio and video airplay and quickly shot to the top of the music charts. "Just the Way You Are" spent more than 20 weeks ranked as No. 1 by *Billboard*, making it one of the longest reigning debut singles in *Billboard* chart history. Mars credits the song's success to its simplicity. "Well, I'm a big fan of songs like Joe Cocker's 'You Are So Beautiful' and Eric Clapton's 'Wonderful Tonight'—songs that go straight to the point. You know, there's no mind-boggling lyrics or twists in the story—they just come directly from the heart. And to me, 'Just the Way You Are' is one of those songs. There's nothing mind-blowing about it. I'm just telling a woman she looks beautiful the way she is—and let's be honest, what woman doesn't wanna hear those lyrics? I mean, that's why I've been singing those kinda songs to get girls since I was nine years old!" "Just the Way You Are" won the 2011 *Billboard* Top Radio Song Award and the 2011 Grammy Award for Best Male Pop Vocal Performance. In addition, the song was nominated for a 2011 Teen Choice Award and several 2011 *Billboard* Music Awards.

The second single from *Doo-Wops & Hooligans* was "Grenade," another chart-topping hit for Mars. "Grenade" was nominated for a 2011 Teen Choice Award and for three 2011 MTV Video Music Awards. With two blockbuster hit songs in a row, Mars became the first male artist in more than a decade to have his two debut singles reach the No. 1 spot on the *Billboard* Hot 100 list. He continued gathering award nominations with his third single, "The Lazy Song," which was nominated for a 2011 MTV Video Music Award and a 2011 Teen Choice Award. Also in 2011, he released *The Grenade Sessions*, a four-song EP of different versions of "Grenade," including remixes and an acoustic track.

Reflecting on the phenomenal success of his first three singles, Mars said, "You know, I don't make a song for the purpose of the radio or anything like that. I just sit down and write a song." *Doo-Wops & Hooligans* sold more than 2.5 million albums and 15 million singles, including more than 4 million downloads. The album was widely praised by music critics. As music reviewer Jody Rosen wrote in *Rolling Stone*, "*Doo-Wops & Hooligans* proves that Mars is a natural—a lavishly gifted melodist (check the surging 'Grenade') and an engaging singer. It's the year's finest pop debut: 10 near-perfect songs that move from power ballads to bedroom anthems to pop-reggae and deliver pleasure without pretension. Call it bubblegum that eats like a meal."

As *New York Times* critic Jon Caramanica wrote, "There's something to be said for learning a wide repertory at a young age, and also to feel no shame in people-pleasing. It's made [Mars] one of the most versatile and accessible singers in pop, with a light, soul-influenced voice that's an easy fit in a range of styles, a universal donor. There's nowhere he doesn't belong."

Becoming a Star

In 2011, Mars built on his success as a songwriter and recording artist by returning to his roots as a talented stage performer. He toured extensively with such acts as Maroon 5, Travie McCoy, and Janelle Monáe. Mars frequently rejected offers to tour with pop music superstars and perform in large arenas. Instead, he chose to play in smaller venues that allowed him to connect with concert-goers.

Critics liked Mars's live performances as much as his records. According to Sarah Rodman, a music reviewer for the *Boston Globe*, "Because the singer-songwriter-producer traffics in the kind of breezy, flyweight soul pop ephemera that lends itself to Top 40 oversaturation—like his infectious hook for Travie McCoy's 'Billionaire'—it's easy to take for granted the craft involved. Every track on his debut album *Doo-Wops & Hooligans* may not be a knockout … but Mars beefed up the thin spots with an entertaining live show that proved he has the skills, heart, and charisma to go the distance." Perhaps the highest praise came from the *Irish Times* in Dublin, Ireland, whose music critic Brian Boyd wrote, "It can be argued that he is already the most outlandishly successful and talented act of his generation. The phrase 'the new Michael Jackson' may only belong in some demented

Mars performing live.

record company press release, but for once we're looking at someone who could potentially have a seismic effect on the music industry."

In addition to the numerous award nominations for his songs, Mars himself has earned a growing list of nods from the music industry and his fans. In 2011, in recognition of his phenomenal success and diverse talents, *Time* magazine named Mars to its 2011 list of the most influential people in the world. He also won two Teen Choice Awards and was nominated for two BET Awards, an NAACP Image Award, four *Billboard* Music Awards, a Nickelodeon's Kid's Choice Award, and a People's Choice Award.

Mars believes that much of his success comes from the time he spent behind the scenes of the music industry. "I realized that you have to go into this industry as an artist with a clear vision and understanding of who you are. Being so young when I was first signed, I never really had a sense of who I wanted to be. Now things are really working out because everything that I'm singing, writing, and composing is really me," Mars said. "There are no tricks.… It's honesty."

Rapper B.o.B. credits Mars's success to a wide-ranging talent in many different aspects of the music industry. As B.o.B. said in *Time* magazine, "Bruno is part of this new wave of musicians who can do everything: sing, play, write, produce. When he performs live, nothing is prerecorded or fudged. It's a straight-up, classic performance. That's so rare these days." In addition to writing and performing his own songs, Mars still writes and produces music for other artists with his partners in the Smeezingtons. "It's hard to put myself in a box. I just write songs that I strongly believe in and that are coming from inside. [There are] no tricks. It's honesty with big melodies," Mars said. "This is what I'm most excited for—taking these songs and traveling them around the world."

HOME AND FAMILY

Mars currently lives in Los Angeles, California.

SELECTED CREDITS

Songwriting

"Long Distance," 2008 (performed by Brandy)
"Right Round," 2009 (performed by Flo-Rida)
"Wavin' Flag," 2009 (performed by K'Naan)
"Nothin' on You," 2009 (performed by B.o.B.)
"Billionaire," 2010 (performed by Travie McCoy)
"Forget You," 2010 (performed by Cee-Lo Green)

Recordings

It's Better If You Don't Understand, 2010 (EP)
Doo-Wops & Hooligans, 2010
The Grenade Sessions, 2011 (EP)

HONORS AND AWARDS

Soul Train Music Awards: 2010, Song of the Year, for "Nothin' on You"
ASCAP Awards (American Society of Composers, Authors and Publishers): 2011, Top Rap Song, for "Nothin' on You"

Billboard Music Award: 2011, Top Radio Song, for "Just the Way You Are"
Grammy Awards: 2011 (two awards), Best Male Pop Vocal Performance, for
"Just the Way You Are" and Best Urban/Alternative Performance, for
"Forget You"
Teen Choice Awards: 2011 (two awards), Choice Music: Breakout Artist
and Choice Summer: Music Star—Male
100 Most Influential People of the Year (*Time* magazine): 2011

FURTHER READING

Periodicals

Billboard, Oct. 9, 2010, p.24; May 2011, p.77
Current Biography Yearbook, 2011
Entertainment Weekly, Sep. 24, 2010
Forbes, June 6, 2011, p.104
New York Times, Oct. 6, 2010, p.C1
New Yorker, Feb. 14, 2011
Rolling Stone, Nov. 25, 2010, p.34; Jan. 20, 2011, p.48; Feb. 12, 2011
Time, Apr. 21, 2011
USA Today, Sep. 16, 2010, p.D1; Dec. 28, 2010, p.D8; Jan. 25, 2011, p.D2
Village Voice, Aug. 18, 2010

Online Articles

www.bluesandsoul.com
   (Blues & Soul, "Bruno Mars: Out of this World," no date)
www.irishtimes.com
   (Irish Times, "Life on Mars: The Future of Pop Music Is on His Way to
   Dublin," Mar. 4, 2011)
www.nytimes.com
   (New York Times, "Bruno Mars in Ascension," Oct. 5, 2010)
www.vibe.com
   (Vibe, "The Big Q&A: Bruno Mars Talks Pop Ascension, Damian Marley
   Collabo, His Song for Nicki Minaj," Oct. 5, 2010)

ADDRESS

Bruno Mars
Atlantic Records
1290 Avenue of the Americas
New York, NY 10104

WEB SITE

www.brunomars.com

Stella McCartney 1971-

British Fashion Designer and Founder of the Stella McCartney Collection of Clothing and Accessories

BIRTH

Stella Nina McCartney was born on September 13, 1971, in London, England. Her father, Paul McCartney, is a British guitarist, singer, songwriter, and former member of the world-famous rock group the Beatles. Her mother, Linda Eastman McCartney, was an American photographer, author, and entrepreneur. McCartney has an older sister, Mary Anna, and a younger brother, James Louis. She also has an older half-sister, Heather, from her mother's first marriage, and a younger half-sister, Beatrice, from her father's second marriage.

YOUTH

As the daughter of famous parents, Stella McCartney grew up in two very different worlds. She enjoyed a normal home life with her family in London, England, but she also travelled the world with her parents and their rock band Wings. Stella was very young when she and her older siblings went on tour with their parents. She spent many nights on the road, sleeping in improvised cribs—usually a hotel dresser drawer lined with pillows and blankets.

> "I went through a period where I thought, 'Do I want to be a landscape gardener? A musician or a photographer? Do I want to do food?' But I really, really loved fashion. It was the thing. I didn't look at films and go, 'Ooh, that's a beautiful planting scheme in the background.' I look at things and say, 'Look at what she's wearing. I love that color.'"

When Stella was ten years old, the family moved from the city to a farm in the rural countryside of West Sussex on the southern coast of England. There they grew their own organic vegetables and raised sheep and horses. Her younger siblings had arrived by then, and she shared one of the small home's two bedrooms with her two sisters. Her brother James slept in the dining room. Within a few years, the family moved to another farm nearby that had a bigger house. In the new house, she was able to have her own bedroom.

Stella grew up with a love of nature and animals. She was a tomboy who never played with dolls, instead preferring to ride her horse, catch frogs, and explore the woods near her family's home. Summers were spent visiting her mother's family in New York. Her parents made sure that their children grew up away from the public world of many celebrity families. Stella knew that her father was a musician, but she did not realize just how famous he was until she saw him perform in concert in Rio de Janeiro, Brazil, for an arena audience of more than 200,000 screaming fans.

As a child, Stella liked to draw pictures of clothing and was interested in fashion design. "I went through a period where I thought, 'Do I want to be a landscape gardener? A musician or a photographer? Do I want to do

Paul and Linda McCartney with daughters Heather (far left), Stella (center), and Mary (right).

food?' But I really, really loved fashion. It was the thing. I didn't look at films and go, 'Ooh, that's a beautiful planting scheme in the background.' I look at things and say, 'Look at what she's wearing. I love that color.'" By the time she was a teenager, she was making her own clothes.

EDUCATION

For elementary and high school, McCartney attended public school in East Sussex, England. She supplemented her regular schoolwork with part-time positions in fashion. In 1986, when she was 15 years old, she worked an internship with renowned French fashion designer Christian Lacroix. Like most fashion interns, McCartney started in the lowest positions. She didn't sew anything or even handle the sewing tools, but she was able to watch and learn about the fashion design industry. Some of her other early learning experiences included a summer position in the fashion department of

British Vogue magazine, internships with other designers, and a stint as a tailor's apprentice in London's exclusive Savile Row. Savile Row shops are known for creating expensive "bespoke" suits for men. Bespoke refers to the tailoring process that is used to create one-of-a-kind custom-fitted suits.

McCartney earned a Bachelor of Arts degree from London's Central Saint Martins College of Art and Design in 1995. Throughout her time there, she struggled against the perception that she was taking advantage of opportunities given to her only because of her parents' fame. McCartney worked hard to prove that she was talented and that she deserved to study at one of the world's most prestigious fashion colleges. Determined to make her own way without help from her parents, she paid for her own expenses by working various jobs, including one as a restaurant dishwasher.

But try as she might, McCartney couldn't always avoid the spotlight. Graduating fashion students traditionally host a runway show to display their final design collections, and McCartney was no different. But unlike most design students, her graduation show was attended by members of the international fashion media. This was due in part to her famous name but also to the models she chose to walk the runway in her show—some of her close friends like Naomi Campbell and Kate Moss, who also happened to be supermodels. McCartney was criticized harshly by her fellow students, who objected to what they saw as an unfair advantage. Her simple response was, "Other students ask their friends to model and I've asked mine." Her graduation show made headlines in fashion publications around the world.

CAREER HIGHLIGHTS

McCartney's career took off immediately after graduation. The media coverage of her student show created great interest in her designs, and she was approached by several large clothing retailers. A Japanese chain with stores in Tokyo and London bought her entire graduation collection, and some of her other early designs were licensed to department store chains in the United Kingdom and the United States.

This initial success was exciting but also presented a big challenge for McCartney. She had constructed all of her early pieces by hand without considering the requirements and restrictions of the manufacturing process needed to make mass market clothing. McCartney had to quickly revise her designs. She made changes in the materials and sewing techniques that she used to create each piece so that the items could be produced in large quantities for department stores. This experience taught her that in order to become a commercial success, she would have to pay more attention to every aspect of her designs. If a finely tailored garment took too long to produce or required costly or rare materials such as antique buttons or lace, then the finished product would be too expensive for most people to buy.

In 1995, McCartney opened a small boutique store in London and launched a line of designs under her own name. The collection was simply called Stella. She made all of the clothing, and she spent a great deal of time involved in the business of running the boutique. She personally ordered materials, cut fabric, sewed the garments, packed them, and sent them to customers. McCartney soon attracted a following among fashion models and celebrities. Her designs were worn by many of her famous friends, including singer Madonna and actors Cameron Diaz and Liv Tyler.

Soon, the business was growing almost faster than McCartney could handle. "I spent so much time on production that the collection was very small. I didn't have time to concentrate on designing." Just when she was at the point of realizing that she would not be able to maintain her design collection by herself, McCartney got an unexpected opportunity that changed her life.

Famed **Vogue** *editor-in-chief Anna Wintour said of McCartney, "What Stella did was to surprise everybody, by very, very quickly developing her own style. It's very much the way she dresses herself, and you can feel her in all the collections she does. We have so few women designers who are really important in the field of fashion, and it's great to have someone like Stella join the ranks."*

An Unexpected Big Break

In 1997, McCartney was named as the creative director of Chloé, a French fashion house that was established in 1952 and known for designing ready-to-wear luxury clothing. She replaced designer Karl Lagerfield, whom the label had just ousted from the position. McCartney was a controversial choice for creative director because she was only 25 years old and had been out of fashion school for less than two years. Many in the fashion industry criticized her as too young and inexperienced and claimed that she was only hired because of her famous name.

McCartney usually chose not to respond to this type of criticism, but now for the first time, she fired back. "I get so sick of this 'my parents' thing. It's been that way my whole life," she declared. "When I did a good drawing at primary school, it was because my dad was famous. Or if I got a part in a

The end of the runway show: McCartney (center) and models react after the presentation of the Chloe 1998 spring-summer fashion collection presented in Paris, October 1997.

school play, it was because Dad was a Beatle. It's the product that counts. People wouldn't want to work with me if they thought I was a complete loser. Women wouldn't wear our clothes. I don't think the Chloé chiefs would be stupid enough to ride a whole company on me because of who my father is. I'm the breath of fresh air that Chloé needs." The fact was, Chloé was dying as a major fashion label, and McCartney was brought in specifically for her fresh, young perspective.

Major fashion designers of ready-to-wear luxury clothing typically present at least two large collections each year: the spring-summer collection and the fall-winter collection. The collection is presented about six months before the season it was designed for, to give time for stores to order the merchandise and for the designer to ship it to stores. Collections are presented in runway shows, where models walk down a runway wearing the outfits as the designer envisioned them. For the most prestigious fashion houses, the audience for the show would usually be the most influential people, including fashion magazine editors, buyers for major stores, celebrities, and others in the fashion industry. Major shows take place in several cities, including New York, Paris, London, and Milan. Reaction by the influential audience members at the runway shows often shapes the response to the collection.

In her new position at Chloé, Mc-Cartney showed ambition, determination, and commitment that quickly earned her a reputation as "Stella Steel." The first Chloé collection launched under her direction was very well received. Her designs revitalized the brand by breaking from the past. McCartney replaced the minimalist, no-frills look of early 1990s fashion with romantic styles that mixed vintage elements with delicate lace and ruffles. She also broke tradition by designing individual pieces of clothing that could be mixed and matched with other fashions. "In the '90s, designers were on this mission to sell 'outfits,' and I felt that was patronizing," she explained. "A woman should be making up her own outfits to reflect her sense of self, instead of becoming what a designer wants her to become."

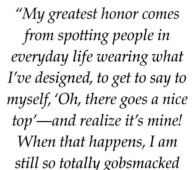

"My greatest honor comes from spotting people in everyday life wearing what I've designed, to get to say to myself, 'Oh, there goes a nice top'—and realize it's mine! When that happens, I am still so totally gobsmacked that anyone would be wearing my clothes."

The look set off a revolution in the fashion world. Under McCartney's direction, demand for Chloé designs rose to an all-time high, and the label was once again the height of fashion. Famed *Vogue* editor-in-chief Anna Wintour said of McCartney, "What Stella did was to surprise everybody, by very, very quickly developing her own style. It's very much the way she dresses herself, and you can feel her in all the collections she does. We have so few women designers who are really important in the field of fashion, and it's great to have someone like Stella join the ranks."

In recognition of her accomplishments as the head of Chloé, McCartney received the prestigious VH1/*Vogue* Designer of the Year award in 2000. Other nominees for the award that year included veteran designers and fashion legends such as Calvin Klein and Miuccia Prada. McCartney's win was remarkable for a designer who had graduated from fashion school only five years earlier.

Launching the Stella McCartney Label

In 2001, McCartney left Chloé and joined Italian luxury fashion label Gucci. There she launched her own fashion label called Stella McCartney. As a strict vegetarian and animal rights activist, she initially turned down the opportunity to work with Gucci because the brand was famous for its use of leather and fur. When she was able to negotiate complete control over her designs, McCartney realized that she might be able to influence the fashion industry from the inside. She wanted to prove that luxury clothing and accessories could be made without animal products.

In her debut collection, McCartney tried to break away from the designs she created for Chloé. She wanted to reinvent her own brand by creating new looks. Her first showing in Paris was a failure—fashion editors hated the clothes as well as the production of the runway show. McCartney's designs were considered inappropriate and even trashy, and her show was criticized for its loud music and flashing lights. "Everything was wrong. It was all a bit messy. I was still finding myself as a person and I was trying to find myself as a brand too quickly. I was nervous and I was overthinking things," she recalled. "I was really freaked out. People think I'm strong, but actually I wanted to crawl away."

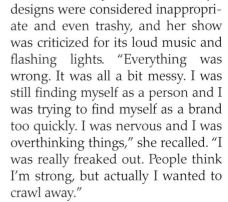

> *McCartney is committed to cruelty-free fashions that use no leather or fur. "There's no excuse for fur in this day and age," she said. "There's nothing fashionable about a dead animal that has been cruelly killed just because some people think it looks cool to wear."*

The failure of her first showing made McCartney even more committed to developing better designs. Her subsequent collections were successful, and by 2002 she had opened the first Stella McCartney store in New York City. Two more stores followed in 2003—in Mayfair, London, and West Hollywood, California. McCartney also began to expand her brand that year, launching her fragrance line with the debut of Stella perfume. In 2004, she began a long-term contract designing a line of active wear for Adidas. In 2005, a special one-time exclusive collection of clothing for retail chain H&M followed. McCartney's line for H&M was placed in 400 stores, and all stores were completely sold out of the entire line in less than an hour.

Branching Out

McCartney continued to expand her collection with the launch of a line of vegan-friendly accessories such as handbags, belts, luggage, jewelry, and shoes. "It's surprising to me that people cannot get their heads around a non-leather bag or shoe," she commented. "They already exist out there,

*McCartney puts the finishing touches on a model backstage at the
Spring-Summer 2005 Paris show in October 2004.*

but unfortunately designers feel that they have to slap a leather trim or sole on them. People need to start looking at the product, and if they like it, that's all that matters. If it has an ethical or ecological edge, that's a huge bonus. We address these questions in every other part of our lives except fashion." McCartney was honored with the Organic Style Woman of the Year Award in 2005. Her commitment to earth-friendly luxury products continued with the launch of CARE, an organic skin care and beauty line. In 2009, she was honored by the Natural Resources Defense Council as a Force for Nature, and *Time* magazine named her among that year's 100 Most Influential People.

By 2010, McCartney had expanded her brand in several directions at once. She created a line of bags and luggage for LeSportsac, launched two more fragrances, and designed a limited-edition collection of children's clothing for GapKids and babyGap stores. She was chosen to design the official outfits for Great Britain's Olympic and Paralympic teams for the 2012 Olympics, marking the first time that a leading fashion designer would create the outfits for both teams.

McCartney also launched Stella McCartney Kids, her own collection of children's clothes, because she had difficulty finding clothing that she liked for her own children. "As a brand with many working parents on the team,

I wanted to create a desirable, fun, wearable kids' collection that was affordable. I feel like all the timeless children's wear is reserved for the expensive brands and that did not sit well with me. Kids and parents, aunts, uncles, friends should all be able to have access to Stella McCartney Kids clothes," she explained. "It's really belittling of the customer to think that anyone from a different price bracket deserves anything less."

> ———— " ————
>
> *"Designing clothes is not about being famous. It's about dressing people, about giving them something that will provide them with a psychological lift as soon as they try it on. I try to design clothes that will make people feel better about themselves."*
>
> ———— " ————

McCartney's retail outlets now include 13 Stella McCartney stores in locations around the world, and her collections are distributed in more than 50 countries. She is widely recognized for her talent in designing accessible clothing that women want to wear. Over the course of her career, McCartney has earned a reputation for her ability to create clothes that are fresh, youthful, and modern. Her designs are often described as down-to-earth and wearable, featuring sharp tailoring and unexpected combinations of old and new elements. She is known for mixing many different types of material in her garments and for her signature color palette of soft shades. "I'm a sucker for muted, dirty, old-looking colors. My whole idea for a color palette is when you open an old chest filled with clothes from the 1920s and they've got enough dirt in them that a once-bright color has been taken down a peg or two."

McCartney's status as a leading fashion designer is firmly in place, and her fans include fashion industry professionals, supermodels, pop musicians, and Hollywood stars. But she still insists that her only job is to "anticipate what a woman needs for her wardrobe." As she explained her approach, "Designing clothes is not about being famous. It's about dressing people, about giving them something that will provide them with a psychological lift as soon as they try it on. I try to design clothes that will make people feel better about themselves.

"I try to create something that I would like and which reflects my personality. You're entering a dangerous area when you try to make things for people because you think that's what they want. You do it because you have a love for it. I'm creating stuff for me and my friends," McCartney said. "In fact my greatest honor comes from spotting people in everyday life wearing what I've designed, to get to say to myself, 'Oh, there goes a

Pieces from the Stella McCartney 2012 Fall-Winter collection.

nice top'—and realize it's mine! When that happens, I am still so totally gobsmacked that anyone would be wearing my clothes."

MARRIAGE AND FAMILY

McCartney married magazine publisher Alasdhair Willis in 2003. They have four children, a son named Miller Alasdhair James Willis (born 2005), a daughter named Bailey Linda Olwyn Willis (born 2006), a son named Beckett Robert Lee Willis (born 2008), and a daughter named Reiley Dilys Stella Willis (born 2010).

MAJOR INFLUENCES

McCartney cites her mother as the biggest influence in her life and career. Linda McCartney was a strict vegetarian and animal rights activist who passed those values and ideals on to her children. "Decisions I've based on my beliefs and upbringing have served me well. I feel in my heart that this is the right way to work and it's the right direction to take our business," McCartney explained. "For me, vegetarianism is based on ethics. It's how I was brought up. My mum was very vocal and we were all educated to understand why we weren't eating meat. But actually, now I look at it from all different angles. I think it's very wrong to have the mass murder, every single day, of millions of animals. I find something wrong with that on a spiritual level, an environmental level, and an ethical level."

As a member of PETA and the Vegetarian Society, McCartney is committed to cruelty-free fashions that use no leather or fur. "There's no excuse for fur in this day and age," she said. "There's nothing fashionable about a dead animal that has been cruelly killed just because some people think it looks cool to wear." But McCartney is also realistic about her ideals. "I'm not by any means perfect. I drive a car. I go on planes. But my philosophy has always been 'Something's better than nothing.'

"I am a fashion designer. I'm not an environmentalist.… If I can make you not notice that it happens to be out of biodegradable fake suede, if I can make you not notice that it hasn't killed cows or goats or unborn baby lambs, then I'm doing my job. There should be no compromise for you as a customer. I don't want to do scratchy, oatmeal-colored things, that defeats the object."

Many of McCartney's clothing designs echo her mother's fashion choices. Some of her signature looks include the mix-and-match styles favored by her mother, such as flowing vintage skirts paired with t-shirts featuring pop-culture designs or high-fashion jackets worn over beat-up blue jeans.

"I think, 'if Mum was here, would she like that?' A lot of the things that I do have originated from Mum's way of throwing things together, sort of old and new and not too self-conscious.… I mean, my mum really was the coolest chick in the world."

HONORS AND AWARDS

VH1/*Vogue* Designer of the Year: 2000, for Stella McCartney for Chloé
Woman of Courage Award (Women's Cancer Research Fund): 2003
Glamour Award: 2004, Best Designer of the Year
Star Honoree, Fashion Group International Night of the Stars: 2004
Organic Style Woman of the Year: 2005
Elle Style Award: 2007, Best Designer of the Year
British Style Award: 2007, Best Designer of the Year
Spanish Elle Award: 2008, Best Designer of the Year
Accessories Council Excellence Award: 2008, Green Designer of the Year
Time 100 Most Influential People: 2009
Glamour Woman of the Year: 2009
Force for Nature Award (Natural Resources Defense Council): 2009

FURTHER READING

Books

Aldridge, Rebecca. *Stella McCartney*, 2011

Periodicals

Current Biography Yearbook, 1998
Ecologist, May 2009, p.50
Flare, Sep. 2008, p.146
Harper's Bazaar, Sep. 2002, p.426
InStyle, Apr. 2004, p. 151; Nov. 2009, p.113
New York Magazine, Mar. 10, 2010
New York Times, Apr. 22, 1997, p.B11; Oct. 22, 2009, p.E4; June 20, 2011
New Yorker, Sep. 17, 2001, p.130
NW, Aug. 13, 2007, p.6
Organic Style, May 1005, p.81
Time, Summer 2006, p.16; Sep. 15, 2008, p.56; Apr. 30, 2010
Washington Post, Oct. 16, 1997, p.B1

Online Articles

www.vogue.co.uk/spy/biographies/stella-mccartney-biography
(British Vogue, "Stella McCartney," May 11, 2011)

ADDRESS

Stella McCartney, Ltd.
Chalegrove House
34-36 Perrymount Road
Haywards Heath
West Sussex RH16 3DN
England

WEB SITE

www.stellamccartney.com

Blake Mycoskie 1976-

American Entrepreneur, Philanthropist, and Founder and Chief Shoe Giver of TOMS Shoes

BIRTH

Blake Mycoskie was born on August 26, 1976, in Arlington, Texas. His father, Mike, is a doctor, and his mother, Pam, is a cookbook author. Mycoskie has two younger siblings, a brother named Tyler and a sister named Paige.

YOUTH

Growing up in Arlington, Mycoskie liked to play golf with his father and brother. The three played as often as they could.

—— " ——

Mycoskie explained his decision to leave school by saying, "I realized I loved doing this. I realized I loved the idea of creating something out of scratch and seeing it work and seeing the benefits of that."

—— " ——

Their golf outings usually included plenty of one-dollar bets with each other to see who could make the longest drive or the best putt.

As a young boy Mycoskie wanted to be a truck driver. He thought it would be cool to drive around the country meeting new people and seeing new places. But by the time Mycoskie was a teenager, he had decided that he wanted to become a professional tennis player. He devoted most of his free time to playing tennis, and he stuck to a rigorous training schedule. All of his hard work paid off when he won a tennis scholarship to Southern Methodist University in Dallas, Texas.

EDUCATION

At Southern Methodist University, Mycoskie studied philosophy and finance and played on the university's tennis team. During his sophomore year, he tore his Achilles tendon. This injury meant that he had to use crutches to walk, and so he was unable to continue playing tennis. When he realized that he couldn't carry his laundry to the dorm's laundry room while he was on crutches, Mycoskie thought he probably wasn't the only student who needed help. He got the idea to start a laundry pick-up and delivery service on the university's campus. His E Z Laundry business grew so quickly that in 1998, he left school to run the company full time.

CAREER HIGHLIGHTS

Becoming an Entrepreneur

The success of E Z Laundry helped Mycoskie realize that he wanted to be an entrepreneur. (An entrepreneur is a person who starts a new business, usually using one's own money and often based on one's own idea.) Mycoskie explained his decision to leave school by saying, "I realized I loved doing this. I realized I loved the idea of creating something out of scratch and seeing it work and seeing the benefits of that."

After just one year, E Z Laundry had expanded to several university campuses and had achieved sales of more than one million dollars. Mycoskie

*A shot from "The Amazing Race": Paige and Blake Mycoskie (both on the left)
arrive at a pit stop in Maui as they pursue the million-dollar prize.*

sold EZ Laundry and moved to Nashville, Tennessee. There he started Mycoskie Media, a successful outdoor advertising company that specialized in
painting huge ads on the sides of buildings. He sold that company after
three years.

In 2002, when Mycoskie was 25 years old, he decided to take a break from
business. He moved to Southern California and was chosen to participate
in the second season of the CBS reality television competition show "The
Amazing Race." His partner for the competition was his sister Paige. The
pair finished in third place. "We lost $1 million by four minutes," Mycoskie
admitted, "and it was all my fault. I epitomized the cliché that men will
never stop and ask for directions."

After being on "The Amazing Race" and seeing firsthand the growing
popularity of reality television programs, Mycoskie decided to start his own
cable television channel. He worked hard to create Reality Central, a channel dedicated to showing reality programs 24 hours a day, seven days a
week. But Mycoskie eventually gave up this idea after competing for three
years against the new Fox Reality Channel. His Reality Central went out of
business in 2005.

Mycoskie's next business venture was an online driver education program
called Driver's Ed Direct. This company was based on the idea that people

would prefer to complete required driver education coursework online, at their own pace, rather than in a classroom setting. Mycoskie founded Driver's Ed Direct in 2005. By 2006, he once again wanted to take a break from business. He decided to travel to South America to visit some of the places that he had glimpsed only briefly during "The Amazing Race."

A Big Idea

Mycoskie's South American vacation included an extended stay in Argentina. There he wanted to learn to play polo, a game in which horseback riders try to score points by using a long-handled mallet to hit a ball through the opposing team's goal. Mycoskie also wanted to experience the nation's culture from the perspective of local residents, so he spent time touring many of Argentina's cities and countryside villages.

Near the end of his vacation there, Mycoskie met two women who were volunteering with an organization that distributed donated shoes to residents of Argentina's poorest villages. These women told Mycoskie about all of the problems that people faced when they had no shoes to wear. Children without shoes were often not able to attend school, because shoes were part of the required school uniform. Foot injuries and diseases were widespread among those who had to walk miles to collect fresh water, food, or other necessities. Mycoskie also learned of a terrible disease called podoconiosis, which results from walking barefoot on soil that contains certain minerals. Podoconiosis causes the feet and legs to become extremely swollen, and the damage is permanent.

As Mycoskie learned more about the women's efforts to provide shoes to those who desperately needed them, he began to see a flaw in their organization's plan. Collecting donations of shoes meant that the organization could not control the supply of shoes that they gave away. They had to rely on whatever they were given, even if the donated shoes were already worn out or in the wrong sizes or styles. Sometimes there were not enough shoes donated for all of the children who needed them, meaning that some children were still without shoes while others were given a pair to wear.

Mycoskie realized that the most effective charitable program would be based on a constant, reliable source of shoes. In this way, everyone who needed a pair could get them. He began to form a plan to create a for-profit business that would be able to provide shoes for those in need. Mycoskie decided that he would start a company to make and sell shoes, with the goal of giving away a pair of shoes for every pair sold. Mycoskie called this new model of charitable giving "one for one," a phrase that highlighted the simplicity of his plan.

Founding TOMS

When he decided to start his one-for-one shoe company in 2006, Mycoskie knew nothing about the shoe business. He enlisted the help of his Argentinian polo teacher, Alejo Nitti, who had also become Mycoskie's close friend. Nitti was an elite polo athlete who also knew nothing about making shoes, but he was excited about the chance to give something back to the people of his country. Mycoskie and Nitti began the company in Nitti's family barn, where they worked to develop the business amongst the family's roosters, iguanas, and donkeys.

Mycoskie wanted to create a shoe for American buyers based on the *alpargata*, the traditional shoe of Argentinian workers and farmers. *Alpargatas* are casual shoes made of soft canvas with a sole made of rope. Mycoskie wanted to make a new kind of *alpargata* that would be more durable and more stylish. He imagined a rubber sole on the bottom instead of rope, soft leather inside, and colorful printed cloth on top. With these modern touches and the addition of arch support, Mycoskie thought the shoes would be both comfortable and appealing to fashion-conscious American shoppers.

——— *"* ———

"On an early drop in Argentina, after the kids got their shoes, they pulled me around their school to a soccer field. It was full of rocks and sticks that would have mangled their feet if they were playing barefoot....While we gave them shoes for health reasons, I realized they viewed them as equipment," Mycoskie explained. *"The most common response we get from the kids and from their parents is that this shoe represents a passport to a better life."*

——— *"* ———

The design of the new shoes began to take shape, but Mycoskie's new company still needed a name. He and Nitti had been working under the slogan "Shoes for a Better Tomorrow." This evolved into "Tomorrow's Shoes" but when this phrase proved to be too long to fit on the shoe labels, it was shortened to simply "TOMS."

Starting Out

To create the first sample shoes, Mycoskie and Nitti enlisted the help of local Argentinian shoemakers. Most of these craftsmen came from families

Two children wearing their new shoes share some food at a soup kitchen in Buenos Aires, Argentina, after receiving their shoes in the first Shoe Drop, 2006.

that had been making *alpargatas* by hand for generations, with traditional skills passed down from father to son. Mycoskie's idea for new *alpargatas* made with modern materials was met with great skepticism. He and Nitti worked hard to convince shoemakers to give the new design a try. In spite of this early resistance to his idea, Mycoskie was certain that he was on the right track. He explained, "The best sign that it's a truly good idea is no one else believes in it."

After a period of experimentation with different materials and a lot of learning by trial and error, Mycoskie eventually had 250 pairs of TOMS shoes to bring back to the United States. He packed all of the sample shoes in a duffle bag and boarded a plane back to Los Angeles to find buyers. Mycoskie had paid for all of the materials and labor with his own money, based only on his confidence in his ability to sell both the shoes and the one-for-one idea behind TOMS. "It was a small project. It wasn't like I, you know, invested hundreds of thousands of dollars and wrote a big business plan and quit my job and all the dramatic things you think of. Now, later I did all those things. But in the beginning it was a very humble start," Mycoskie said. "People get scared because they think they need a giant loan, but you can start on a very small scale."

Back in Los Angeles, Mycoskie set up a web site to explain the TOMS one-for-one concept and to sell shoes directly to consumers. He also began trying to find stores where TOMS could be sold. But without any knowledge of the retail shoe industry, Mycoskie ran into problems trying to break into the market. Sales were nearly nonexistent until the *Los Angeles Times* ran a story about TOMS and Mycoskie's one-for-one giving program. Sales skyrocketed overnight and the TOMS web site logged more than 2,000 orders in one day. With less than 200 pairs of shoes in stock, Mycoskie scrambled to come up with a plan.

After contacting all 2,000 customers to inform them of a delay in shipping their orders, Mycoskie quickly returned to Argentina to oversee the manufacture of 4,000 pairs of shoes. At that time, TOMS was still relying on local shoemakers working in very small shops. Some of these craftsmen could only complete one part of the whole shoe. Mycoskie and Nitti spent most of their time driving back and forth across Buenos Aires, delivering materials and partially constructed shoes to the next person in the TOMS assembly line.

By the time Mycoskie brought the next batch of shoes back to the United States, TOMS had been featured in *Vogue, Elle, People, Teen Vogue, Time,* and *O* magazines. Mycoskie fielded calls from stores including Nordstrom, Urban Outfitters, and even Whole Foods. Within the first six months, 10,000 pairs of TOMS shoes were sold.

The First Shoe Drop

Mycoskie had planned the first shoe giveaway, or shoe drop, to take place after 10,000 pairs were sold. "When I first used the term 'shoe drop,' someone asked me if anyone ever gets hurt. They thought we were flying by and dropping boxes of shoes, which could be problematic. But that's not what happens." Mycoskie returned to Argentina with his parents, his brother and sister, and several close friends. They travelled the countryside in a bus, stopping in remote rural villages to distribute free shoes to those in need.

Mycoskie described that first shoe drop as one of the most important moments in his life. "The children had been told we were coming, and our local organizers had informed us of the needed shoe sizes. The kids, anticipating a new pair—or their very first pair—of shoes were so eager for our arrival that they would start clapping with joy when they spotted the bus rolling into town. I broke down in tears many times. 'Oh, my God,' I thought, 'This is actually working.' At each stop I was so overcome with emotion that I could barely slip the first pair of shoes on a child without crying with love and happiness."

Mycoskie with recipients of TOMS shoes.

"On an early drop in Argentina, after the kids got their shoes, they pulled me around their school to a soccer field. It was full of rocks and sticks that would have mangled their feet if they were playing barefoot. Growing up as an athlete, I remember being stoked about any new gear that would improve my game. While we gave them shoes for health reasons, I realized they viewed them as equipment," Mycoskie explained. "The most common response we get from the kids and from their parents is that this shoe represents a passport to a better life.

"When I returned from that first shoe drop, I was a different person. I also realized that TOMS wasn't going to be just another business for me. It was going to be my life, in the best sense.... All at once it made a living for me and everyone who worked at TOMS, it brought me closer to the people and places I loved, and it offered me a way to contribute something to people in need. I didn't have to compartmentalize any of my life's ambitions: personal, professional, or philanthropic. They all converged in a single mission."

Mycoskie sold his remaining shares of Driver's Ed Direct and invested the money in expanding TOMS. He hired his first paid employees, including several people who had experience in the shoe industry. Together, this new team dedicated themselves to furthering the one-to-one mission of TOMS.

A Big Break

Mycoskie decided early on that TOMS would have no advertising budget. Instead, the company would rely only on social networking and the comments of satisfied customers. "Most footwear companies spend a fortune on traditional advertising, athlete endorsements, TV commercials and billboards," he explained. "The only way TOMS works is if we spend no money on traditional advertising. All of our marketing comes from social media and word of mouth." But the biggest publicity break still came in the form of a commercial on national television—though TOMS didn't pay for it.

In 2009, AT&T approached Mycoskie with a proposal to feature TOMS in one of its commercials. The commercial focused on the one-for-one concept behind TOMS and how TOMS used AT&T services to run its worldwide operations. The commercial ran for 12 weeks during popular shows such as "Dancing With the Stars," "American Idol," and "Survivor." The commercial was also shown on video screens in 5,000 New York City taxi cabs. It is estimated to have reached hundreds of millions of people. Demand for TOMS shoes exploded after this commercial was aired. As a result, TOMS was able to give away more than 300,000 pairs of shoes in 2009—more than twice as many as were given away in the company's first three years combined.

TOMS has expanded its operations significantly since 2009 and now works with local community health organizations around the world. "Our global shoe giving is now accomplished through humanitarian organizations with deep roots in the communities in which they operate," Mycoskie commented. "They serve children in a holistic way, through health, education, clean water, and more. And they integrate our shoes into their programs for even greater impact. Their ongoing presence means we can get shoes to kids again and again as they grow.

"When I started TOMS, people thought I was crazy," Mycoskie ad-

"I started TOMS with half a million dollars. If I had taken that money, bought shoes, and distributed them to needy kids, I would have been able to do it only once. But with my business plan, which allows us to give one pair away for each pair we sell, it's a sustainable venture. We can give shoes away every year, grow the business, and help more kids."

mitted. "In particular, longtime veterans of the footwear industry argued that the model was unsustainable or at least untested—that combining a for-profit company with a social mission would complicate and undermine both. What we've found is that TOMS has succeeded precisely *because* we have created a new model. The giving component of TOMS makes our shoes more than a product. They're part of a story, a mission, and a movement anyone can join."

Becoming a Social Entrepreneur

Over the course of his career as the head of TOMS, Mycoskie has changed the way in which businesses can participate in charitable giving. In 2010, TOMS was named as one of the Ten Most Innovative Retail Companies by *Fast Company* magazine. Mycoskie's work has also become a model and an inspiration for a new type of businessperson, called a social entrepreneur. Social entrepreneurs are people who start businesses with the dual goal of making money and helping others at the same time. "I think the term 'social entrepreneur' is very relevant because I believe you can do well by doing good," Mycoskie argued. "TOMS is a for-profit business, and it's important that we have profit so we have sustainability.… The nice thing about TOMS is it being a for-profit business, we're continuing to sell shoes so we can continue to give shoes.

"We've also made it clear to our customers from the very beginning that our company is not like most others in the social-impact sector—we are a *for-profit* company. Our goal is to help people and to make money doing it. We have never hidden that from anyone and in so doing have paved the way for a new type of social venture," Mycoskie explained. "I started TOMS with half a million dollars. If I had taken that money, bought shoes, and distributed them to needy kids, I would have been able to do it only once. But with my business plan, which allows us to give one pair away for each pair we sell, it's a sustainable venture. We can give shoes away every year, grow the business, and help more kids."

Since its creation in 2006, TOMS has given away millions of shoes in 23 countries around the world, including the United States, Argentina, Ethiopia, Haiti, and South Africa. "As we've grown our giving has become more focused on specifically preventing diseases for kids in certain areas of the world," Mycoskie said. "TOMS started as a social experiment but it quickly became a shoe company. Now, it's moving more toward a movement. I want to not only be giving shoes around the world and fulfilling our one-to-one promise but working with doctors and local governments to eradicate Podo [podoconiosis] in 15 to 20 years."

Mycoskie announcing a new One for One program—TOMS eyewear.

In 2011, Mycoskie announced that TOMS was expanding the one-for-one giving model with the launch of the TOMS line of eyewear. For every pair of sunglasses or eyeglasses sold, TOMS will provide medical treatment, prescription glasses, or eye surgeries to a person in need. Also in 2011, he published *Start Something That Matters*. This book outlines his approach to business and provides advice and inspiration for aspiring social entrepreneurs. Mycoskie is donating half of his profits from the sales of the book to his Start Something That Matters Fund, which he created to encourage organizations and projects that make a positive impact on the world.

Mycoskie spends most of his time travelling, either delivering shoes on shoe drops or speaking about his business philosophy. "Often, I'm traveling around the country to speak at companies and universities about our business model. I love teaching people what we do. My goal is to inspire the next generation of entrepreneurs and company leaders to think differently about how they incorporate giving into their business models.

"Increasingly, the quest for success is not the same as the quest for status and money. The definition has broadened to include contributing something to the world and living and working on one's own terms," Mycoskie said. "Start now. Start by helping other people—anyone you can. Do something simple. You don't have to start a business or big initiative right

———— " ————

"The definition [of success] has broadened to include contributing something to the world and living and working on one's own terms," Mycoskie said. "Start now. Start by helping other people—anyone you can. Do something simple. You don't have to start a business or big initiative right away—you can begin just by changing you mindset. Commit to seeing the world through the lens of how you can initiate meaningful change."

———— " ————

away—you can begin just by changing you mindset. Commit to seeing the world through the lens of how you can initiate meaningful change.

"Almost everyone has a passion for something, but sometimes we have trouble saying what it is. It's surprisingly easy to lose touch with our true passions—sometimes because we get distracted with everyday living; sometimes simply because in the usual stream of small talk or transactable business, no one ever asks us about our dreams. That's why it's so important that you first find a way to articulate your passion *to yourself.* When you discover what your passion is, you will have found your story as well."

HOME AND FAMILY

Mycoskie lives on a sailboat in Marina Del Rey, California, but he is rarely there. "I'm home about five or six days a month, and the rest of the time I'm on the road."

HOBBIES AND OTHER INTERESTS

When he is not working, Mycoskie enjoys fly fishing, surfing, sailing, and writing. "Almost every morning I write in my journal. I've been keeping it for a long time—I've filled more than 50 books. I write about what's going on in my personal and spiritual life or what's going on at work. It helps me keep things in perspective, especially when things get crazy or I get stressed or we have obstacles. When I go back a month later and read what I was feeling, I realize that it wasn't that big of a deal—we got through it. And that helps me prepare for the next time that I deal with difficult stuff."

Mycoskie also enjoys reading and is especially interested in biographies. "I read quite a bit when I'm on the road. I've read a lot of business biographies.… The great thing about biographies is the subjects have already been successful, so they're not insecure about their failures."

HONORS AND AWARDS

People's Design Award (Smithsonian Institution Cooper-Hewitt National
Design Museum): 2007
Award for Corporate Excellence (U.S. Secretary of State): 2009

FURTHER READING

Books

Mycoskie, Blake. *Start Something That Matters*, 2011

Periodicals

Business Week, Jan. 26, 2009, p.18
Fortune, Mar. 22, 2010, p.72
Inc., June 2010, pg.112
Los Angeles Times, Apr. 19, 2009; June 12, 2011
Men's Health, Sep. 2008
Newsweek, Oct. 11, 2010, p.50
Texas Monthly, Sep. 2008, p.34
Time, Jan. 26, 2007
Time for Kids, Mar. 2, 2007, p.6
Vogue, Oct. 2006

Online Articles

bigthink.com/ideas/1121
(Big Think, "Blake Mycoskie on Becoming an Entrepreneur," Apr. 28,
2008)
www.cnn.com
(CNN, "Blake Mycoskie: Sole Ambition," Sep. 26, 2008; "These Shoes
Help Others Get a Step Up," Mar. 26, 2009)
cox.smu.edu/web/guest/blake-mycoskie
(Cox School of Business, "Blake Mycoskie," no date)
www.fastcompany.com
(Fast Company, "Blake Mycoskie, Founder and Chief Shoe Giver of
TOMS Shoes," Oct. 14, 2010)
laist.com
(LAist.com, "PhiLAnthropist Interview: TOMS Shoes Founder Blake
Mycoskie Plans to Give Away 300,000 Pairs in 2009," Apr. 15, 2009)
www.openforum.com
(OpenForum.com, "Trendsetter: TOMS Founder Blake Mycoskie on
Starting a Movement," Oct. 5, 2011)

ADDRESS

Blake Mycoskie
TOMS Shoes, Inc.
3025 Olympic Blvd., Suite C
Santa Monica, CA 90404

WEB SITES

www.startsomethingthatmatters.com
www.toms.com/blakes-bio

Michele Norris 1961-

American Journalist, Host of the National Public Radio Show "All Things Considered," and Author of the Memoir *The Grace of Silence*

BIRTH

Michele L. Norris was born on September 7, 1961, in Minneapolis, Minnesota. She grew up in Minneapolis with her mother, Elizabeth Norris, and father, Belvin Norris Jr., who were both postal workers.

YOUTH

Dealing with Racial Issues

Norris grew up in a time of transition in race relations in the United States, an issue that affected her childhood and her professional career. The civil rights movement was making significant progress in changing "Jim Crow" laws, which had begun in the late 1800s and lasted until the 1960s. These Jim Crow laws, which were founded on the legal principle of "separate but equal," made it legal to discriminate against African Americans. These laws forced the segregation of the races and created "separate but equal" public facilities for blacks and whites. Restaurants, bathrooms, railroad cars, movie theaters, schools, and other public places were segregated, with one set of facilities for whites and another set of facilities for blacks. Although these separate facilities were called equal, in reality those for blacks were miserably inadequate. African Americans usually attended dilapidated, impoverished schools with underpaid teachers. After leaving school, their opportunities for work were often just as limited. These were the conditions for many African Americans at that time, especially in the South.

> "What I remember was a wonderfully integrated community where we had friends from all across the color line. What I experienced in south Minneapolis was distinctly at odds with what I saw on the television regarding integration. It just seemed so easy when I looked around my neighborhood. I didn't realize it was anything but easy for my parents. When they first moved in, every family whose property line touched ours moved out."

Norris knew that her parents had faced racism and had suffered under these Jim Crow laws. Her father had lived in Birmingham, Alabama, an area of the Deep South that was extremely segregated. If he wanted to go downtown, he would have to plan his trip in advance and take food with him because he might not be able to sit at a restaurant due to his race. "My parents were very careful how they presented those stories," she explained. "They told me some things and they didn't tell me others." Norris spent many summers in Birmingham, and her parents would tell her to be careful. She remembers "getting a lecture … not to look white people in the eye, to be careful when we moved about downtown, never to draw at-

Jim Crow laws, like those that forced this African-American man to drink from the "colored" water cooler, were common when Norris's parents were growing up in the first half of the 20th century.

tention to yourself, to make sure you were dressed a certain way when you always went out in public spaces."

When Norris was growing up in Minnesota, Norris's segregation was still common. At that time it was rare for black and white people to live on the same block, and her family was the first black family on her street. Sandy Banks, a writer for the *Los Angeles Times,* described Norris's upbringing like this. "Norris' parents were the first blacks on their block in Minneapolis. Her father was a Navy vet, raised in Birmingham before civil rights arrived, so determined not be looked down upon that he woke early on snowy days to shovel the driveway and sidewalk before his white neighbors looked outside. Her mother was a fourth-generation Minnesotan who hailed from the only black family in a small northern town." Norris said her parents always made it a point to keep their lawn nice and dress well when going out. She called her family a "Model Minority," determined to prove that their family was as respectable and responsible as any white family. It worked: the whole family got along well with their white neighbors in Minnesota.

Norris doesn't recall very much racial tension in her childhood. However, she still experienced some teasing because of her race. In school, kids made hurtful comments, telling her she had a "kinky little Afro." Nonetheless, she knew that segregation was more deeply entrenched in other parts of the country. "Growing up, I was shielded from what happened," she recalled. "What I remember was a wonderfully integrated community where we had friends from all across the color line. What I experienced in south Minneapolis was distinctly at odds with what I saw on the television regarding integration. It just seemed so easy when I looked around my neighborhood. I didn't realize it was anything but easy for my parents. When they first moved in, every family whose property line touched ours moved out."

Life at Home

When Norris was young, her father had an interesting way of getting her attention. He came home from work every day and called out, "MEE-shell!" She liked the way it sounded so much that she began saying her name the same way, and her family and friends soon caught on.

> *Throughout her childhood, Norris was encouraged to read the newspaper every day. "I grew up in a household where my parents devoured the papers and the evening news and instructed their children to do the same, up to quizzes at the dinner table."*

Throughout her childhood, Norris was encouraged to read the newspaper every day and to value education. "I grew up in a household where my parents devoured the papers and the evening news and instructed their children to do the same, up to quizzes at the dinner table." Her father said she could do anything, as long as she focused on her studies.

Even though Norris's family was respected in her neighborhood and her parents were supportive, family life was not perfect. Her parents divorced when she was a teenager. "There was a silent tornado in our home, and it led to the breakup of my parents' marriage," she said. She lived with her father after the divorce.

EDUCATION

Norris attended Washburn High School in Minneapolis, where she was part of the cheerleading squad and wrote for her high school student newspaper. Her parents' support of her studies helped her to succeed in school and to decide to attend college.

Norris with her father, Belvin Norris Jr.

Norris started college in 1979 at the University of Wisconsin-Madison, where she studied electrical engineering. She was part of a national program called InRoads, which gave scholarships to minority students who did well in math and science classes in high school. While she was studying electrical engineering, she had a C average. Her heart was not in her work, and she said she found her studies "fascinating but isolating." She needed to change direction, and she thought she should study writing. "I always tell the story that, when I was in engineering, I would wind up rewriting the word problems, then maybe I would get to solving the problem," she said. "Engineering was interesting, but it was a diversion. Although it did help me because it teaches you to think logically. So it wasn't a waste of time. But I've always been interested in writing and storytelling and ultimately found my way to my calling."

In 1982, Norris transferred to the University of Minnesota, where she studied journalism. She wrote for the university newspaper, the *Minnesota*

Daily, at that time the fourth-largest student-run paper in the state. In 1985, before she graduated, she dropped out of school to take a job in journalism. She later returned to school and completed her journalism degree at the University of Minnesota in 2005.

CAREER HIGHLIGHTS

Starting Out as a Journalist

Throughout her career, Norris has worked in a variety of jobs in journalism—in television, newspaper, and radio. In 1985, while still attending college in Minnesota, she landed her first professional job—at the CBS TV station, WCCO, where she was an assistant in the newsroom. She didn't work there long, though. In 1985, she landed a job with the *Los Angeles Times.* Over the next eight years, from 1985 to 1993, Norris worked for three of the largest newspapers in the country: the *Los Angeles Times*, the *Chicago Tribune,* and the *Washington Post.*

While working for the *Los Angeles Times*, Norris lived in San Diego, California. One of her first stories focused on why the prices of necessary goods, like food and prescriptions, were much higher in poor neighborhoods than in wealthier ones. Her stories focused on social problems, such as poverty and education. At the *Chicago Tribune,* Norris continued writing about education. She wrote stories about a high school principal's damaged property and a teachers' strike at a local school system. Her passion for education stories flourished at the *Tribune.* At the *Washington Post,* Norris again wrote about social issues. One of her first stories was about a six-year-old boy who lived with his drug-addicted mother. Their house was identified by police as a house where drugs were sold. Norris earned national respect for the series of stories on the boy. She also won the Livingston Award in 1990, which is given to American journalists under the age of 35. The articles were reprinted in the collection called *Ourselves Among Others: Cross-cultural Readings.*

In 1993, Norris was surprised to be asked by ABC News to be a television news correspondent, which means she was an on-screen reporter. She had never worked on TV before, but she jumped at the chance to try something new. Besides, she was proud to bring more racial diversity to the program. "I know what it's like to turn on the TV and not always see people who look like you," she said. The chance to change the face of television gave her work a higher purpose.

During her time with ABC, Norris was a Washington-based correspondent for "World News Tonight," "20/20," "Nightline," and "Good Morning

Norris at the microphone in the NPR studios while on the air.

America." Her stories focused mostly on education, inner-city issues, poverty, and the nation's drug problems. While working at ABC she earned an Emmy Award, an award given for excellence in television, for her coverage of the terrorist attacks on September 11, 2001. She worked at ABC News until 2002.

Moving to National Public Radio

In 2002, Norris became the co-host of "All Things Considered," the longest-running program on National Public Radio (NPR). The job offer came out of the blue. By this point, she was married with children, a big factor in her decision. "It was one of those rare opportunities, in which you could take a gigantic step forward in your career without taking a concomitant step away from your family," she explained. "I was actually able to stay closer to home because I'm tied to the studio, which meant I would be traveling less." "All Things Considered" is a two-hour news program that airs each weekday on public radio stations around the country during the afternoon drive time, about 4:00 to 6:00 p.m. The award-winning show has been on the air for more than 40 years and now counts more than 13 million listeners. Each show includes the biggest news stories of the day mixed with interviews, commentaries, reviews, and human-interest stories, all enlivened with sound. The show has three hosts, but only two hosts are on at any time; Norris co-hosts "All Things Considered" with Robert Siegel and Melissa Block.

When Norris first started, she was concerned about moving from TV to radio. The staff at NPR really thought about the training she would need and helped her adapt to the responsibilities of being a radio host. One of her bosses, NPR vice president Bruce Drake, praised her ability to report on a wide range of stories. "She's comfortable reporting on everything from Washington politics to popular culture," Drake said. News correspondent Gwen Ifill, who appears on public television (Public Broadcasting System, or PBS), agreed with Drake. "She can see beyond the story to the human element almost instantly. You feel like you're eavesdropping on a private conversation," Ifill said.

------ " ------

"There's something incredibly powerful about the intimacy of radio and the way that it plays on the listener's imagination," Norris argued. *"A soldier knocks on someone's door to deliver bad news. You can describe that in print. You can show that in television. But somehow when you combine the descriptive powers and the ambient sound that they use so well here at NPR to take the listener to that place, it's a very powerful medium."*

------ " ------

Norris is the first African-American woman to host a program on NPR, and she likes having another chance to bring racial diversity to the media. She enjoys radio in particular. Norris has suggested that radio is more intimate than print or television journalism because it forces the audience to pay more attention to the story in order to fully understand what is being reported. In print journalism, readers often read the first paragraph to get a general idea of the story, and then they stop and move on to something else. In television journalism, viewers focus on the pictures and video clips more than what the correspondent is saying. Radio journalism is different. "Radio is wonderful because you use the storytelling and descriptive writing that you call upon in print and you enhance that with sound," she declared. "There's something incredibly powerful about the intimacy of radio and the way that it plays on the listener's imagination. A soldier knocks on someone's door to deliver bad news. You can describe that in print. You can show that in television. But somehow when you combine the descriptive powers and the ambient sound that they use so well here at NPR to take the listener to that place, it's a very powerful medium." It's not only radio in general that Norris enjoys; it's being a part of NPR itself. "I meet someone and after they figure out what I do, they tell me how much NPR means to them."

Norris has said that working at NPR is the hardest job she has ever had. She likes that "All Things Considered" includes the excitement of live reporting on current events, as well as the high production quality of taped pieces about ongoing issues. NPR has given Norris the opportunity to interview famous and influential people, including Oscar winners, American presidents, military leaders, and astronauts. She enjoys the variety.

One story, in particular, led Norris down a new path. During the 2008 presidential campaign between then-Democratic candidate Barack Obama and Republican candidate John McCain, she helped with a series called "The York Project: Race and the '08 Vote." She worked with another NPR reporter, Steve Inskeep, host of the NPR show "Morning Edition." She and Inskeep reported on 15 hours of discussions among a group of voters living in York, Pennsylvania. They wanted to explore the attitudes of York voters regarding race, since Obama was the first black politician to be so close to becoming president. Norris and Inskeep wanted to know how voters' views about race would affect their votes. The two reporters found that the election was an opportunity for voters to reconsider their racial views. "People started talking about race in a different way," Norris said. For their work on "The York Project: Race and the '08 Vote," she and Inskeep were co-winners of the Alfred I. duPont-Columbia University Award.

Returning to Writing

Inspired by the 2008 presidential election, Norris began considering taking a break from NPR in 2009 in order to write a book that focused on people's thoughts about race in general—not just in relation to politics. "I thought there was an interesting conversation about race taking place in the country … and I wanted to swim in that conversation for a while." Norris thought the book would be called *You Don't Say: On Matters of Race and the Consequences of Silence.* "People talk about race one way in public and they often talk about it in a different way in private," she explained, "and I just want to pull back the curtain a little bit." The book was supposed to be a collection of essays about other people.

When Norris began looking into the country's experiences with racism, she also began listening to her own family's stories, especially those about her parents and grandparents. But Norris didn't hear those stories directly from the people involved; instead, she heard them from other family

Norris with her "All Things Considered" co-host, Robert Siegel, reporting on the presidential campaign on Super Tuesday 2009.

members who were tired of hiding the truth. The more she learned, the more she had to know. "It was like the elders were going through a period of historic indigestion," she observed. "All these stories and things they had kept to themselves were coming up and coming out." She kept asking questions and decided that, instead of writing about the country's history with racism, she would write a book about her own family's history. Their stories would relate to racial issues in the United States in general, but she would be able to learn about her own family along the way.

Writing Her Father's Story

Learning her family stories wasn't always fun. One morning, Norris was having breakfast with an uncle, who was saying that young people don't understand how much older generations had sacrificed in order to change racial attitudes to the point that the United States could elect a black president. In the middle of the conversation, her uncle calmly said, "Well, you know your father was shot." Norris was washing dishes at the time, and she was so startled that her knees buckled and she sank to the floor. Her father never told his children or his wife about being shot by a white police officer in Birmingham, Alabama, after returning from serving in the U.S. Navy during World War II. "Perhaps it was too difficult to go back there in his mind," Norris said. So she took it upon herself to learn what he never told her.

Norris decided that her book would become a memoir about her family. Since her father had died more than 20 years before she learned the truth, she had to rely on her investigative skills to find more. She tracked down police records, military documents, and interviews. Once she started researching, she couldn't stop. She learned that the shooting occurred in February 1946, two weeks after her father returned from military service in World War II. Norris's father, uncle, and a friend were in Birmingham, Alabama, an area where racism was deeply entrenched. In this segregated community, the men were in the lobby of a building that housed black professionals.

While Norris's father and the other two black men were waiting for an elevator, two white policemen blocked the elevator entrance with nightsticks. They knocked her father down and put a gun to his chest. Instinctively, Norris's father pushed the gun down just in time for the policeman to shoot him in the leg instead of the chest. Norris's father was not the only one attacked in this way—in a week, about six black veterans were killed by white police officers in Birmingham. Her father's story represents a sordid episode in U.S. history—an example of the United States showing contempt for a group of people who had served in the military to defend their country. "My father was part of a group of men who fought for their country," Norris later said. "They did their part. They participated in the fight for democracy in foreign lands, and they got this crazy idea that they could get a taste of it back home. They loved a country that didn't love them back." She knew this would be an important story to include in her book.

"My father was part of a group of men who fought for their country," Norris said. "They did their part. They participated in the fight for democracy in foreign lands, and they got this crazy idea that they could get a taste of it back home. They loved a country that didn't love them back."

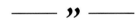

Revealing Her Grandmother's Past

Norris never expected that she would learn something about her grandmother that would startle her as much as her father's story. Iona Brown, Norris's grandmother, was remembered as a well-dressed, elegant woman who was proud of her race. When Norris learned that her grandmother worked as an Aunt Jemima look-alike in the late 1940s and early 1950s, traveling throughout the Midwest to give demonstrations about how to use the pancake mix, Norris was stunned. It may not sound like a bad thing to be an Aunt Jemima look-alike, but in the 1940s and 1950s, Aunt Jemima was drawn to look like a slave woman. The fact that Brown presented herself as a slave did not match the image of the woman Norris remembered from her childhood. When she found a newspaper article with a picture of her grandmother in slave clothes, she didn't know what to think.

Norris's mother never told anyone about this because she was ashamed about the racist presentation of Aunt Jemima. However, Norris was not immediately embarrassed for her grandmother. "I was fascinated because I thought, well wait a minute, she was traveling to small towns in the 1950s, when women didn't really travel at that time," she said. When she dug deeper into this aspect of her grandmother's past, she found that Brown used her tour as Aunt Jemima to give white people a different impression of black people. "She took a job that could so easily have been demeaning, but she did it with great dignity in her own way," Norris said. Brown would focus on the children at her presentations. If they became comfortable with black people, she hoped, they might avoid the racist attitudes of their parents. Norris said her grandmother served as a sort of cultural representative, giving white people a positive view of black people. She was proud to use Brown's story as a part of her memoir.

Norris's work changed the way she thought about her elders. Her research led her to question how well children know the people who raise them? She was unhappy to realize that she hadn't known the most life-changing moments of her father's and grandmother's lives. On top of that, family members who had known these facts kept them from her for most of her life. She understood their silence, though. "It's not because they're dishonest. It's because they want the best for us," she reasoned. "They don't want to weigh us down with their own frustrations." She doesn't look back in anger, but in wonder. She remembered her family's philosophy: "If you want your babies to soar, you don't put rocks in their pockets."

Reaction from the Public

Norris decided to call her book *The Grace of Silence,* which was published in 2010. She settled on the title after learning about her father's shooting. Her father and the other members of her family inspired her because "they set aside their personal grievances in order to help America become a better place, and that is an incredibly graceful act," she said. She hopes the book will help readers think about their own family's history and help them realize the importance of sharing what they have been through.

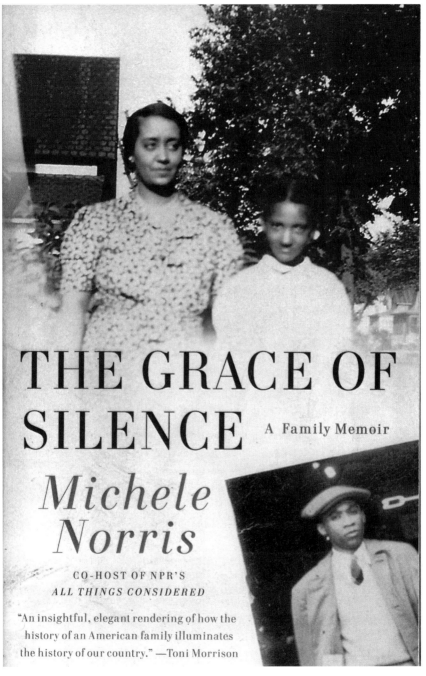

THE GRACE OF
SILENCE   A Family Memoir

*Michele
Norris*

CO-HOST OF NPR'S
ALL THINGS CONSIDERED

"An insightful, elegant rendering of how the
history of an American family illuminates
the history of our country." —Toni Morrison

Norris's family memoir The Grace of Silence *describes her own
life experiences as well as those of her elders.*

Critics pointed out that Norris used all of her journalistic skills to write *The Grace of Silence.* She interviewed and investigated her way to the truth, just as she has in her career as a journalist. However, because she was investigating her own family's past, there was a deeper appreciation for the type of work she was doing and its emotional toll. As Donna Seaman wrote in *Booklist,* "The result is an investigative family memoir of rare candor and artistry that dramatically reveals essential yet hidden aspects of African-American life.... Norris looks at both sides of every question while seeking truth's razor-edge. But she is also a remarkably warm, witty, and spellbinding storyteller, enriching her illuminating family chronicle with profound understanding of the protective 'grace of silence' and the powers unchained when, at last, all that has been unsaid is finally spoken."

> "
> *"People talk about race one way in public and they often talk about it in a different way in private,"* Norris explained, *"and I just want to pull back the curtain a little bit."*
> "

Many critics appreciated the way that Norris combined her personal story with events in U.S. history, as in this comment from Lisa Bonos in the *Washington Post.* "She blends the story of her childhood—and her quest to fill in its gaps—with a wider view of Southern race relations immediately following World War II, a period often overshadowed by history's focus on the Martin Luther King era of the 1960s," Bonos wrote. "'What's been more corrosive to the dialogue on race in America over the last half century or so,' Norris asks, 'things said or unsaid?' Her struggle to answer that question becomes a powerful plea to readers to doggedly pursue their families' story lines. She reminds us that speaking candidly about race in America starts not at the president's teleprompter but at our own dinner tables." That view was echoed by Sandy Banks in the *Los Angeles Times.* "Norris displays strong reporting skills and an eye for detail as she renders perfectly a familiar slice of middle-class Midwestern life for black families in the 1960s, when every household had a Bible, a World Book Encyclopedia, and two parents constantly admonishing us to dress well, speak properly, act right," Banks wrote. "Norris has a reporter's instinct for knowing when to get out of the way and let people talk—whether it's the retired white policeman wistfully touting the benefits of segregation or the elderly black woman angrily unpacking ugly memories of Birmingham. She paints a painfully intimate portrait of that city and that era, making clear the toll that official segregation took on 'aspirational Negroes.'"

Race Cards and Other Projects

After Norris published *The Grace of Silence,* she went on a promotional tour, giving readings and discussing the book in both small and large settings. At these events, she gave out postcards and asked people to write about race in just six words. She viewed the cards as a way to start a conversation on this difficult topic. To her surprise, she was overwhelmed with cards and emails. "All over the country people who came to hear about my story wound up telling me theirs," she said. "Despite all the talk about America's consternation or cowardice when it comes to talking about race, I seemed to have found auditorium after auditorium full of people who were more than willing to unburden themselves on this prickly topic."

Norris has commented on the cards and her decision to post many of them on her website. "They are thoughtful, funny, heartbreaking, brave, teeming with anger, and shimmering with hope. Some will make you smile. Others might make you squirm. And there are a few that might make you wonder why they deserve a place on my website's Race Card Wall. Here's the answer. If the intention is to use these cards to get a peek at America's honest views about race, then I must try to honor those people who offer up candor, even if what they share is unsavory or unacceptable in some people's eyes."

In 2011, Norris announced that she was taking a leave of absence from hosting "All Things Considered." Her husband, Broderick Johnson, took a position as a senior advisor in the campaign to re-elect President Barack Obama. Journalists are expected to be impartial and objective in their reporting, and it would be considered a conflict of interest for her to cover political stories related to the campaign while her husband was working for one of the candidates. Norris decided to temporarily leave her hosting duties at "All Things Considered," but she wasn't leaving NPR. She planned to continue to report and produce stories on a special projects basis.

MARRIAGE AND FAMILY

Norris lives in Washington, D.C., with her husband, Broderick Johnson, and their two young daughters. Norris met Johnson at a political party in the early 1990s. She later interviewed him and invited him to a board-game party. During a round of the game Scattergories, Norris and Johnson found themselves giving all the same answers. "I looked at him and said, 'I'm marrying that man,'" she said. Norris married Johnson in 1993. She has two small children and an adult stepson, Broddy—Johnson's biological son—who lives in Washington, D.C.

HOBBIES AND OTHER INTERESTS

In Norris's free time, she enjoys gardening, writing, and listening to jazz music. It isn't always easy for her to find time to balance her job and her family. Norris said juggling her career and home life can be "like juggling chainsaws … while riding a skateboard … during a tornado." Working at NPR has given her more time at home, since she doesn't have to travel as much. When she is home, her favorite thing to do is cook for her family.

WORKS

The Grace of Silence, 2010

HONORS AND AWARDS

Livingston Award for Young Journalists (Mollie Parnis Livingston Foundation): 1990, for coverage of six-year-old living in a crack house
Emmy Award: 2001, for coverage of 9/11
Outstanding Achievement Award (University of Minnesota): 2006
Salute to Excellence Award (National Association of Black Journalists): 2006, for coverage of Hurricane Katrina
Outstanding Women in Marketing & Communications Award (Ebony Magazine): 2007
Alfred I. Dupont-Columbia University Award (Columbia University): 2008, for excellence in broadcasting (with Steve Inskeep)
Journalist of the Year (National Association of Black Journalists): 2009, for coverage of 2008 presidential campaign
25 Most Influential Black Americans (Essence Magazine): 2009
Power 150 List (Ebony Magazine): 2009

FURTHER READING

Periodicals

Bookmarks, Jan.-Feb. 2011, p.55
Current Biography Yearbook, 2008
Los Angeles Times, Sep. 28, 2010, p.D2
New York Times Book Review, Jan. 30, 2011, p.26
Washington Post, Oct. 6, 2010, p.C1

Online Articles

www.csmonitor.com
  (Christian Science Monitor, "NPR's Michele Norris on Her Family's Hidden History," Sep. 23, 2010)

www.journalismjobs.com
    (Journalism Jobs, Medill-Northwestern University, "Interview with
    Michele Norris," Apr. 2003)
www.npr.org
    (National Public Radio, "Michele Norris: Host, *All Things Considered*,"
    Dec. 2, 2009; "10 Questions: NPR's Michele Norris," 2009)
www.washingtonpost.com
    (Washington Post, "All Things Reconsidered: NPR's Michele Norris Tells
    Her Family's Complete Story," Oct. 6, 2010)

ADDRESS

Michele Norris
NPR
635 Massachusetts Avenue, NW
Washington, DC 20001

WEB SITES

www.michele-norris.com
www.npr.org/people

Jaden Smith 1998-

American Actor and Star of the Hit Movie *The Karate Kid*

EARLY YEARS

Jaden Christopher Syre Smith was born on July 8, 1998, in Los Angeles, California. His father, Will Smith, is an actor, producer, and rapper. His mother, Jada Pinkett Smith, is an actor and singer. Smith has a younger sister, Willow, and an older half-brother, Trey, from his father's first marriage.

Smith made his acting debut when he was five years old. He appeared as Reggie in six episodes of the television comedy

"All of Us," which aired on the CW network from 2003 to 2007. Smith was homeschooled by his mother until 2009, when he began attending classes at the New Village Leadership Academy in Calabasas, California. He enjoys playing video games, listening to rap music, writing rap lyrics, and hanging out with his friends. "I go to the movies a lot, you know? I love vampire movies. I like kung-fu movies too. I love horror movies and comedies too. *Twilight*, all those, I love those movies."

MAJOR ACCOMPLISHMENTS

The Pursuit of Happyness

Smith landed his first movie role when he was just seven years old in the drama *The Pursuit of Happyness*, based on a real-life story. Smith played Christopher, the five-year-old son of Chris Gardner, the film's main character (played by his father, Will Smith). *The Pursuit of Happyness* tells the story of how Gardner became a self-made millionaire after working his way out of poverty. When his wife leaves him and their young son, he struggles to make ends meet but soon finds himself unemployed and with no place to live. He and his son survive on the streets of 1980s San Francisco by sleeping in shelters or bus stations, bathing in public restrooms, and finding refuge wherever they can. With few job prospects, Gardner decides to take an unpaid internship at a prestigious stock brokerage firm. Though there is no salary, he hopes the position will lead to a paying job that could provide a secure future for himself and his son. The story focuses on one pivotal year in the lives of Gardner and his son as they endure the hardships of being homeless while working towards a better life.

Smith became interested in the role of Christopher after his father had been cast as Gardner. In talking to his father about the movie, Jaden asked if he might be able to play the part. His father said, "You don't just get the job because you're my kid. You'll have to audition like everyone else, and you may not get it, that's how it works." Jaden went to the audition with his mother, where he learned that he would be competing for the role against 100 other young actors. The film's director liked Smith, and he got the part.

> *"I go to the movies a lot, you know? I love vampire movies. I like kung-fu movies too. I love horror movies and comedies too. *Twilight*, all those, I love those movies."*

The Pursuit of Happyness was a major hit when it was released in 2006. The

Smith in a scene from The Pursuit of Happyness
with his father and co-star, Will Smith.

movie was the top box office moneymaker during its opening weekend
and received glowing reviews from movie critics. Reviewers were particularly impressed with Jaden Smith's performance. The role was challenging
for an actor as young as Smith was at the time, and the story was difficult
and emotional as father and son struggled with life on the streets. A *USA*

Today movie reviewer praised Jaden's ability to show the complexity of the character. "He plays this resilient boy in a way that indicates an innate intelligence. He seems to sense how down-and-out they are; you can read his fear, and even his occasional anger. He's not a sunny Pollyanna of a child, but he's not a cynic, either. It's as if he realizes that the only way to survive is to keep his head down and persevere."

Smith's portrayal of Christopher earned a 2007 MTV Movie Award for Breakthrough Performance and a 2007 Teen Choice Award for Choice Movie: Chemistry, which he shared with his father. That same year, Smith was also nominated for a Teen Choice Award for Choice Movie: Breakout Male, an NAACP Image Award for Outstanding Supporting Actor in a Motion Picture, and a Black Reel award for Best Breakthrough Performance.

Appearing alongside his father in *The Pursuit of Happyness* convinced Jaden that he wanted to pursue a career as an actor. "After I did that movie, I was like 'yeah, wow, this is something that I might like to do.'" Smith went on to play the role of eight-year-old Jacob in the 2008 remake of *The Day the Earth Stood Still*. In this science fiction drama, an alien space traveler named Klaatu and a robot named Gort arrive on Earth and threaten to destroy the human race. With all life on Earth at stake, Jacob and his stepmother must convince Klaatu that humans deserve to survive. For his performance as Jacob, Smith won a 2009 Saturn Award for Best Performance by a Younger Actor from the Academy of Science Fiction, Fantasy and Horror Films.

In 2009, Jaden and his sister Willow became youth ambassadors for Project Zambi, a charitable program that works to raise awareness of the millions of children who are affected by the AIDS epidemic in Africa. "Willow and I joined Project Zambi to represent all the kids out there who want to make the world a better place," he said. "We want to encourage kids everywhere to lend a hand and join us in spreading the word about how much children who have been orphaned by AIDS in Africa need our help."

The Karate Kid

When he was 12 years old, Smith won his first starring role, in the remake of the 1984 movie *The Karate Kid*. This martial arts drama focuses on the story of Dre, played by Smith. After his father dies, Dre and his mother leave Detroit and move to Beijing, China, for her new job. Dre was popular and had a lot of friends in Detroit, but in China he is an outcast. He struggles to understand the Chinese culture and society and finds that he just doesn't fit in. It seems that all of Dre's new schoolmates know kung-fu,

Scenes from The Karate Kid.

and the school bullies don't hesitate to use their skills against him. A particularly savage beating motivates Dre to begin studying martial arts. Dre's teacher is a former martial arts master (played by Jackie Chan) who is now the maintenance man at the apartment building where Dre lives. As Dre's fighting skills progress, he decides to enter a tournament where he ultimately must prove himself by facing the relentless bully Cheng.

Smith couldn't wait to get to work on the movie. "I've always really been interested in martial arts. I started taking karate when I was three. So when my dad mentioned this idea to remake the movie, there's no way I was going to pass that up!" To prepare for the role, Smith began an intense martial arts training program. He practiced three hours a day for four months before filming started. The fight scenes were his favorite parts of the movie. "The tournament at the end of the movie was the most fun and the hardest to shoot because I had to constantly fight every day. It was exhausting. But it was also really cool."

All of Smith's hard work paid off, and *The Karate Kid* became an international phenomenon when it was released in 2010. The movie was a box office sensation that grossed more than $350 million worldwide and made Smith an instant star. Though the movie received mixed reviews from critics, Smith was praised for his talents as an actor and a martial artist. A reviewer for *Film Journal* described *The Karate Kid* as a "formulaic but savvy reboot of the four-film series [that] makes for a solid children's movie, bolstered by exotic locales and a genuinely talented young star.… Smith seems at once in conscious control and emotionally spontaneous. He has a great, subtle way of showing the doubt beneath Dre's blustery bravado, and of seeming like a genuinely irritating 12-year-old and not a ham-fisted, obnoxious movie 12-year-old."

Smith's performance in *The Karate Kid* was recognized with a host of award nominations. *Entertainment Weekly* named Smith a Top Celebrity of 2010. In 2011, he was nominated for an NAACP Image Award for Outstanding Actor in a Motion Picture, an MTV Movie Award for Biggest Badass Star, and two Teen Choice Awards for Choice Summer Movie Star: Male and Choice Red Carpet Fashion Icon: Male. Smith also shared with Jackie Chan a People's Choice Award nomination for Favorite On-Screen Team. Smith won a 2011 Young Artist Award for Best Performance in a Feature Film—Leading Young Actor and shared the 2011 BET Young Stars Award with his sister Willow.

Along with starring in *The Karate Kid*, Smith also recorded "Never Say Never," a song on the movie's soundtrack that he performed with pop singer Justin Bieber.

Jaden with his family: mother Jada Pinkett Smith,
sister Willow Smith, and father Will Smith.

Other Projects

Smith's next movie is *One Thousand A.E.*, a science fiction adventure story in which he will once again star opposite his father. The two play a father and son who explore a vacant Earth after their space ship crashes on the planet. *One Thousand A.E.* is scheduled for release in 2012.

After *One Thousand A.E.*, Smith plans to appear in more movies. "Yes, definitely, I want to be an actor. I want to travel around the world and meet new people. It's pretty cool going to different cities and seeing different stuff." But he isn't limiting himself to just acting, and would also like to record more music. "I just like rapping, and I've always been good at poetry," he claimed. "I love both. I'll be writing rhymes in a director's chair when I'm older."

HONORS AND AWARDS

MTV Movie Award (MTV): 2007, Breakthrough Performance, for *The Pursuit of Happyness*

Teen Choice Award: 2007, Choice Movie: Chemistry, for *The Pursuit of Happyness*, shared with Will Smith

Saturn Award (Academy of Science Fiction, Fantasy & Horror Films): 2009, Best Performance by a Younger Actor, for *The Day the Earth Stood Still*

Top Celebrity of 2010 (*Entertainment Weekly*): 2010
Young Artist Award (Young Artist Foundation): 2011, Best Performance in
    a Feature Film—Leading Young Actor, for *The Karate Kid*
Young Stars Award (BET): 2011, shared with Willow Smith

SELECTED CREDITS

The Pursuit of Happyness, 2006
The Day the Earth Stood Still, 2008
The Karate Kid, 2010

FURTHER READING

Periodicals

Daily Variety, Apr. 5, 2011, p.1
Ebony, July 2010
Entertainment Weekly, Apr. 23, 2010, p.70; Dec. 10, 2010, p.84
Jet, Dec. 15, 2008, p.38; June 28, 2010, p.28
USA Today, June 4, 2010

Online Articles

www.biography.com
    (Biography, "Jaden Smith," no date)
www.kidzworld.com
    (Kidzworld, "Jaden Smith Bio," no date)

ADDRESS

Jaden Smith
Overbrook Entertainment
450 North Roxbury Dr., 4th Floor
Beverly Hills, CA 90210

WEB SITE

www.jadensmith.com

Emma Stone 1988-

American Actress and Star of the Hit Movies
Zombieland; *Easy A*; *Crazy, Stupid, Love*; and *The Help*

BIRTH

Emily Jean Stone was born on November 6, 1988, in Scottsdale, Arizona. Her mother, Krista, was a homemaker. Her father, Jeff, operated his own construction company. She has
one brother named Spencer. Stone changed her first name to
Emma when she became an actress, in order to avoid confusion with another actress named Emily Stone.

YOUTH

Stone grew up in Scottsdale, Arizona. As a young girl, she enjoyed watching movies with her parents, especially comedies. "My dad showed me the classics—*Animal House, The Jerk*—and I connected comedy to my happiness," she explained. "I think I was drawn to comedy originally because when I was really young, by the time I was eight I had seen movies like *The Jerk, Animal House,* and *Planes, Trains & Automobiles* with my dad, and I knew them by heart. I loved them and my dad loved them, and we would laugh together, and I would think, 'This is love.' I just wanted to make people feel like that." She also shared her mother's love of sketch comedy. "My mom loved 'Saturday Night Live' and Gilda Radner. She would do Gilda Radner impressions and she showed me old 'Saturday Night Live' shows when I was about seven."

> ———— " ————
>
> *"By the time I was eight I had seen movies like* **The Jerk, Animal House,** *and* **Planes, Trains & Automobiles** *with my dad, and I knew them by heart. I loved them and my dad loved them, and we would laugh together, and I would think, 'This is love.' I just wanted to make people feel like that."*
>
> ———— " ————

When she was 11 years old, Stone began acting in community theater productions with the Valley Youth Theater in Phoenix, Arizona. She appeared in 16 plays, including *Alice in Wonderland, Cinderella, The Little Mermaid,* and *The Princess and the Pea.* She was also a member of an improvisation comedy troupe. (Improvisation is a form of comedy that is not planned or scripted. Instead, performers respond to situations, characters, and each other by making things up as they go along.) Stone has said that her childhood experiences performing comedy helped her later in her acting career. "I think every kid should have access to something like that, because it's not only great training for acting, but for life. Learning improv skills is kind of like being on the debate team, you know? You learn life lessons." She also enjoyed writing and performing her own original sketch comedy pieces.

Though Stone always knew that she wanted to be a performer, it took a while for her to figure out what kind of performing artist she most wanted to be. Throughout her childhood, she explored different performance styles, as she explains here. "I wanted to do comedy, and then I thought I wanted to do theater, so I wanted to do musical theater, and then I took voice lessons for like eight years, and I sucked at singing, so I was like, 'Alright, nevermind.'" By the time she was a teenager, Stone had decided on a career as an actor.

Stone decided when she was 14 years old that she wanted to move to Hollywood. When she told her parents what she wanted to do, at first they would not even consider allowing it. In order to show her parents how serious she was about going to Hollywood, Stone carefully prepared a persuasive argument. "When I was 14 years old, I made this PowerPoint presentation, and I invited my parents into my room and gave them popcorn. It was called 'Project Hollywood 2004' and it worked."

Stone at the 2011 Teen Choice Awards.

EDUCATION

Stone attended Sequoya Elementary School and Xavier College Preparatory High School in Arizona. Her schooling changed at age 15, when she moved to California and began pursuing a full-time career as an actor. At that time, Stone left traditional high school and enrolled in online classes so that she could complete her school work on a more flexible schedule that allowed her to go to more auditions.

CAREER HIGHLIGHTS

In January 2004, when she was 15 years old, Stone moved to Los Angeles with her mother. She hired an acting agent and began auditioning for roles. After eight months, she still had not landed any acting jobs. Stone took a part-time job at a bakery that made treats for dogs. Her job was to bake dog cookies, and she soon discovered that she had no talent for the work. "I think three people called my specific dog cookies inedible to their dogs. I'm not a super-talented dog baker."

Stone's first year in Los Angeles was more difficult that she imagined it would be. "It's definitely a shock to go from being 15 and in high school to working. There's no real cushion there. There's no preparation at all. You learn by doing," she explained. "I don't know why I had to do it right then.... I was having breakdowns—'What am I doing? I'm 15 years old! I have no friends! I'm not in school—why did I need to do this?' But I kept pushing through it, and I'm so glad I got rejected for so long because things fall into your lap when you least expect it.... So follow your gut. Your gut will tell exactly what to do when you need to do it."

Starting Out

In 2005, Stone got her first acting job. She was cast as a contestant on a proposed VH1 reality competition show called "In Search of the New Partridge Family." The original "Partridge Family" television showed aired in the 1970s. It was about a single mother and her five children who perform together as pop musicians. The winners of the new VH1 competition would be cast in a remake called "The New Partridge Family" TV show. Stone filmed the pilot episode of the reality competition, but VH1 decided not to create the series. Though this show did not work out, she said the experience was extremely valuable. "I met a lot of people that ended up having a big effect on my life. It all kind of changed from there."

"It's definitely a shock to go from being 15 and in high school to working. There's no real cushion there. There's no preparation at all. You learn by doing," Stone explained. "I was having breakdowns— 'What am I doing? I'm 15 years old! I have no friends! I'm not in school—why did I need to do this?'"

One of the people that Stone met during that time became her new manager and helped her get more acting jobs. She soon landed guest roles on popular TV shows like "Malcolm in the Middle," "The Suite Life of Zack and Cody," and "Medium." She auditioned for the role of Claire on "Heroes" but lost the part to actress Hayden Panettiere. Stone recalls being devastated when she was not chosen for that role. She learned the news by overhearing a conversation while she waited outside the audition room. "I could hear that, in the other room, a girl had just gone in and they were saying, 'You are our pick.... On a scale of one to ten, you're an 11.' I went home and just had this meltdown."

Though she did not get the part on "Heroes," the rejection motivated Stone to try even harder on her next audition. She was cast in a 2007 TV series called "Drive," a drama-action series about a group of people who were competing in an illegal cross-country road race. The show only lasted one season, but the experience ultimately led to Stone winning her break-out role in the movie *Superbad*.

Becoming a Movie Actor

Stone's first movie role was in the 2007 comedy *Superbad*, the story of two high school seniors who want to do something cool and daring before they graduate. Although they are underage, they decide to try to buy alcohol and bring it to a party thrown by Jules, played by Emma Stone. On the way to Jules's house, the two join forces with another friend, meet up with a couple of strange local police officers, and get into a series of misadventures. *Superbad* was a box office hit that quickly became a cult classic.

Stone was thrilled to be part of the movie. "The script was so hysterical to me, so I was just excited to be a part of something that was that funny and in line with my humor, because that's so rare." Though she had only a supporting role, playing Jules gave Stone the chance to show off her acting talent and comedic abilities. Her performance in *Superbad* earned her the 2008 Young Hollywood Exciting New Face Award.

After *Superbad*, Stone began to receive more job offers, leading to roles in a string of movies. In the 2008 movie *The Rocker*, she played Amelia, a bass guitar player in an amateur rock band. That same year, she appeared in *The House Bunny* (2008), the story of a former Playboy bunny who becomes a sorority house mother and proceeds to give all of the sorority members beauty and lifestyle makeovers. Stone played Natalie, the sorority's quick-witted president. Then in 2009, she appeared in the romantic comedy *Ghosts of Girlfriends Past*. This romantic comedy tells the story of a man who tries to talk his brother out of getting married and is subsequently visited by three ghosts, one of which is played by Stone. The ghosts give him glimpses of his past, present, and future romantic relationships, causing him to think about the way he has been living his life. These roles broadened Stone's appeal and helped her to land her first starring role in the action movie *Zombieland*.

Zombieland

In the 2009 comedy-horror movie *Zombieland*, Stone played Wichita, one of the survivors of a catastrophe that turned most humans into zombies. With the world in ruins, Wichita joins up with three other survivors for a road trip across America to find a place that is free from zombies. The movie became an instant cult hit, and Stone was nominated for a 2010 Teen Choice Award for Choice Movie Actress: Comedy. A writer for movie review web site Rotten Tomatoes said, "Emma Stone is rapidly carving a niche for herself as a young actress with good comic chops."

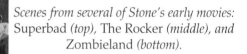

Scenes from several of Stone's early movies:
Superbad *(top),* The Rocker *(middle), and*
Zombieland *(bottom).*

For Stone, the experience of filming an action movie presented new challenges. "I'm shockingly terrible at action movies. I tore my muscle three days in just running, and then I was limping around everywhere.... I was limping like a zombie. I'm dead serious. We're running from zombies, and I'm limping in the same fashion that they limp. It was just awful." Stone also found herself genuinely frightened in some of the movie's scenes, even though she knew the zombies weren't real. "On the second day, [costar Abigail Breslin] and I had to be chased by something like 30 zombies and it was two o'clock in the morning and I was really overtired. I started getting these paranoid thoughts that one of them was really crazy. I was like, 'How do you know you can trust these people?!' So we're running from these people and shooting at them and in my mind I'm thinking, 'What if one of them snaps and attacks me?' I got myself into a paranoid tizzy about it."

> —— " ——
>
> *"I'm shockingly terrible at action movies," Stone said about filming* Zombieland. *"I tore my muscle three days in just running, and then I was limping around everywhere.... I was limping like a zombie. I'm dead serious. We're running from zombies, and I'm limping in the same fashion that they limp. It was just awful."*
>
> —— " ——

Easy A

Stone's next project was the 2010 teen comedy *Easy A*. In this movie, Stone starred as Olive Penderghast, an uncool high school student who gains a bad-girl reputation after one tiny lie grows bigger each time it is repeated on the gossip grapevine. Olive soon finds that she has been branded as the school slut, although she is actually still a virgin. Instead of trying to correct the misunderstanding, Olive decides to take advantage of her new status by working the school's rumor mill. Stone said the message of *Easy A* is that gossip and rumors are not always true. "No matter how true something may seem, we don't really know if it's fact or fiction."

Easy A became a hit with moviegoers and critics as well. "Whatever else it accomplishes, the sassy high school comedy *Easy A* commands attention for the irresistible presence of Emma Stone, playing a good girl who pretends to be bad," Stephen Holden wrote in the *New York Times*. "Her performance is the best of its type since Alicia Silverstone's star turn several high school generations ago in Amy Heckerling's 1995 hit *Clueless*." Re-

Easy A *was Stone's first big film.*

viewer Elizabeth Weitzman predicted a successful future for Stone in the *New York Daily News*: "Expect to hear much more about Emma Stone, who's thoroughly charming as misguided heroine Olive Penderghast."

For her performance in *Easy A*, Stone earned a 2010 Golden Globe nomination for Best Performance by an Actress in a Motion Picture Comedy or Musical. She was nominated for 2011 MTV Movie Awards for Best Female Performance and Best Line from a Movie, and she won the MTV Movie Award for Best Comedic Performance. During its "Thankful Week," MTV News named Stone "the actress we're most thankful for in 2010." Stone also won a 2011 Teen Choice Award, for Choice Movie Actress: Romantic Comedy.

In fall 2010, Stone fulfilled one of her lifelong goals by hosting "Saturday Night Live." "I've never been so happy in my entire life," she said of that experience. "Walking into Studio 8H and seeing pictures of Gilda Radner and Bill Murray and Steve Martin and Jan Hooks and Eddie Murphy and Molly Shannon and everyone I've ever admired in this exact room on this exact stage—I mean, beyond."

Stone followed the success of *Easy A* with a starring role in the 2011 romantic comedy *Crazy, Stupid, Love*. This movie tells the story of Cal (played by Steve Carell), a man who tries to enter

"The Emma Stone Character represents a kind of young American female role (and role model) in precious short supply these days—one who likes herself and cherishes her options," film critic Lisa Schwarzbaum wrote in **Entertainment Weekly.** *"That a generation of young women and men are learning from the real Stone's bright example is more valuable still."*

the dating world after his wife leaves him. He finds a mentor, Jacob (played by Ryan Gosling), who is willing to teach him how to pick up women. The lessons seem to be going well until Jacob meets Hannah, played by Stone. Hannah is the one woman for whom Jacob's playboy techniques are completely ineffective. Things get complicated as relationships become intertwined and everyone struggles to figure out what they really want. Though the movie received mixed reviews from critics, Stone was praised for her performance. Movie reviewer David Denby wrote in the *New Yorker* that Stone "has a direct, clearheaded way about her that suggests the confidence of a potential star. She's the strongest thing in the movie."

Also in 2011, Stone made a cameo appearance in the romantic comedy *Friends with Benefits*. She appeared in one scene, in which she broke up with the lead character Dylan, played by Justin Timberlake.

The Help

Stone's first dramatic role was in the highly anticipated 2011 movie *The Help*, a film adaptation of the 2009 bestselling novel of the same name by Kathryn Stockett. The book was a worldwide phenomenon that ranked on bestseller lists for more than 100 weeks. The story of *The Help* takes place in the early 1960s in Jackson, Mississippi. It focuses on the relationships between African-American maids and their white employers during the turbulent and tense early days of the civil rights movement. Stone plays Eugenia "Skeeter" Phelan, an ambitious young writer who wants to learn about the life experiences of the maids who work for her friends. Though it was unheard-of and incredibly risky for whites and blacks to talk about the racial tensions of that time, Skeeter manages to convince two maids to let her interview them. The story unfolds as the women begin to speak openly about their lives.

Though *The Help* was a bestselling novel and many readers eagerly awaited the movie version, a great deal of controversy also surrounded the project. *The Help* was praised by many film critics but heavily criticized by others. Some in the African-American community objected to the story as an oversimplification of the terrible racial discrimination that occurred in the time and place shown in the movie. Others thought the story was too condescending and implausible and did not provide a complete picture of the times or the lives of the African-American characters, especially black women.

"Many audiences, especially African-American viewers, are exhausted with seeing black actresses as maids. It was a role to which many black actresses were regulated to for decades, and *The Help* brings back old Hollywood memories that some would rather forget," Clay Cane wrote for BET. "Regardless of mammy stereotypes, *The Help* needed some help with its janky, watered-down storyline and its Disneyfied version of the Jim Crow South. Predictably, the movie focuses more on the rich, racist characters versus the heart of the film, the impoverished domestic servants and their untold stories. There should've been fewer Southern tea parties and poolside gatherings and more of the gritty realities of being a maid in the '60s. For a film that is set in pre-civil rights Mississippi, it is too bright and cheery, cheapening the horrific experiences of legalized racism…. In moments, the film works, but overall it was another clichéd civil rights film

Scenes from The Help.

with all of the typical elements: the ultra-racist evil white person, ... the sympathetic Southern woman suffering from white guilt, a sassy black rebel and a flock of obedient Negros."

But many others enjoyed and defended the film, including Peter Rainer, a critic for the *Christian Science Monitor*. "*The Help* too often feels like a civics lesson.... I would defend *The Help*, simplistic though it is, against the charge that some have leveled against it for being 'patronizing.' It's true that, by framing the maids' stories through Skeeter's lens, the film implicitly overvalues the historical contribution of whites to the civil rights movement [but] ... there are not so many stirring, full-fledged black characters on the screen, particularly black female characters, that we should feel it necessary to downgrade the few that we have by playing the blame game."

Amidst the controversy, Stone's performance was praised as believable and honest. Matt Stevens, a critic for *E! Online,* wrote that the movie provides "a clear understanding of Southern Culture and manages to stitch together the many patches of this crazy quilt, even if some pieces don't fit perfectly.... Stone, too, is stellar as the plucky, progressive Skeeter." David Denby observed in the *New Yorker*, "Stone makes it clear that Skeeter's break with her friends is produced as much by ambition for a hot literary subject as by moral disapproval. She is one of the few actresses playing a working writer who have actually seemed like one." As Owen Gleiberman wrote in *Entertainment Weekly*, "I've loved Stone as a wide-eyed comic sprite, but here, playing a young woman more no-nonsense than anyone around her, she doesn't just sparkle—she holds the movie together."

Other Plans

Stone has earned a reputation as a talented comedic and dramatic actor and is widely recognized as a rising star among younger actors. Lisa Schwarzbaum, a film critic for *Entertainment Weekly,* summarized her star potential by describing the types of roles she typically chooses. "The Emma Stone Character represents a kind of young American female role (and role model) in precious short supply these days—one who likes herself and cherishes her options. That a generation of young women and men are learning from the real Stone's bright example is more valuable still." Her next movie will be *The Amazing Spider-Man*, a new version of the super-hero story that is expected to be in theaters in 2012. She will co-star as Gwen Stacy, Spiderman's girlfriend.

While she enjoys acting in movies, Stone also enjoys working behind the scenes. "I really want to produce eventually because I love movies so much," she said. "It's really incredible to see something that you got to be a part of become something that people really respond to and are grateful is around." Stone has achieved her childhood dream of becoming an actor, and she is ready for whatever the future brings. "I rely on my instincts and intuition, and I feel it's so imperative for people to follow not the path, but their path."

HOME AND FAMILY

In 2009 Stone moved to New York City, where she lives with her dog Alfie. "I feel like I'm home for the first time, I really do. Arizona never felt like home, except for my family, and L.A. never felt like home except for my friends. And here, feels like the place I was always meant to live."

HOBBIES AND OTHER INTERESTS

In spite of her early failure as a baker of dog cookies, baking is now a serious hobby for Stone. She plans to work an internship at a gourmet bakery someday.

SELECTED CREDITS

Superbad, 2007
The Rocker, 2008
The House Bunny, 2008
Ghosts of Girlfriends Past, 2009
Zombieland, 2009
Easy A, 2010
Crazy, Stupid, Love, 2011
Friends with Benefits, 2011
The Help, 2011

HONORS AND AWARDS

Young Hollywood Awards: 2008, Exciting New Face, for *Superbad*
MTV Movie Awards: 2011, Best Comedic Performance, for *Easy A*
Teen Choice Award: 2011, Choice Movie Actress: Romantic Comedy, for
    Easy A

FURTHER READING

Periodicals

Entertainment Weekly, July 9, 2010, p.50; Apr. 22, 2011, p.56; Aug. 12, 2011,
    p.32
Teen Vogue, Sep. 28, 2008, p.195; Oct. 2010, p.76

Us Weekly, Sep. 27, 2010, p.72
Vanity Fair, Aug. 2011, p.83
Vogue, Mar. 2011, p.538

Online Articles

www.accesshollywood.com
   (Access Hollywood, "Rising Star: Emma Stone," June 4, 2008)
www.ew.com
   (Entertainment Weekly, "Emma Stone's Hot Summer: With *The Help*
   and *Crazy, Stupid, Love* in Theaters, the Actress' Career Is on Fire. Allow
   Us to Fan the Flames," Aug. 5, 2011)
www.nowtoronto.com
   (Now Toronto, "Emma Stone," Sep. 9, 2010)
www.rottentomatoes.com
   (Rotten Tomatoes, "Emma Stone Talks *Zombieland*—RT Interview," Oct.
   7, 2009)
www.snmag.com
   (Saturday Night, "Emma Stone: Coolest Chick We Know," July 2008)

ADDRESS

Emma Stone
William Morris Endeavor Entertainment, LLC
9601 Wilshire Blvd., 3rd Fl.
Beverly Hills, CA 90210

WEB SITES

thehelpmovie.com/us
www.sonypictures.com/homevideo/easya

Abby Wambach 1980-

American Soccer Player with the U.S. Women's National Team and Gold Medalist at the 2004 Olympic Games

BIRTH

Mary Abigail Wambach (pronounced WAHM-bahk), known as Abby, was born on June 2, 1980, in Rochester, New York. Her parents, Peter and Judy Wambach, own a garden supply store. Abby is the youngest of seven children in her family. Her siblings, who range from 2 to 11 years older, are Beth, Laura, Peter, Matthew, Patrick, and Andrew.

YOUTH

As the youngest member of a very active family, Abby grew up playing a variety of rough-and-tumble games on the cul-de-sac where they lived. "My mom would literally lock us out of the house and say go play," she recalled. "We wouldn't be able to come in, not even to pee."

Starting when Abby was five or six, her brothers would dress her up in makeshift hockey pads and make her stand in front of a net while they fired slapshots at her. She also demonstrated her fearless nature in neighborhood basketball and football games. "One of the first experiences where I knew she'd be better than most was a game of football," her brother Matthew remembered. "I threw the ball to one of the neighbors and Abby tackled him. She got up and he was on the ground, groaning. She was 11 or 12."

> *As the youngest member of a very active family, Abby grew up playing a variety of rough-and-tumble games on the cul-de-sac where they lived. "My mom would literally lock us out of the house and say go play," Wambach recalled. "We wouldn't be able to come in, not even to pee."*

Abby was first introduced to soccer when her sister Beth checked out a book from the library about the sport. She joined her first girls' soccer team at the age of four. After she scored 27 goals in 3 games, however, Abby was moved to a boys' team. "Boys aren't going to let you win, no matter what," she noted. "I had to learn to use my body because the boys were stronger than I was." Even after changing leagues, Abby continued to excel on the soccer field. As she got older and went back to girls' leagues, she played for the Rochester Spirit Soccer Club and was selected to the Olympic Development Team U-16 National Team.

EDUCATION

Wambach attended Our Lady of Mercy, an all-girls Catholic high school in Rochester. She starred in both soccer and basketball, playing varsity all four years in each sport. On the soccer field, she scored 142 goals during her high school career, including an amazing 39 goals as a senior in 1997. She was selected as a High School All-American in both 1996 and 1997, and as a senior she was named High School Player of the Year by the Na-

Wambach playing for the University of Florida Gators in 2000.

tional Soccer Coaches Association of America. Wambach enjoyed representing Mercy on the soccer field, although she regrets that her high school team never won a state championship. Mercy made it to the state finals in 1997, but the team blew a 3-goal lead and lost the title. "That in a lot of ways motivates me to continue being better because that's something I know I didn't accomplish," she stated.

After graduating from high school in 1998, Wambach accepted a scholarship to play soccer at the University of Florida. She made an immediate impact as a freshman, scoring 19 goals to help the Gators claim the National Collegiate Athletic Association (NCAA) national championship. During her senior season in 2001, Wambach led all NCAA Division I players with 31 goals and 13 assists for 75 points (a player's points in soccer are calculated by doubling the number of goals scored and then adding assists). Her performance helped lift the Gators to an appearance in the Final Four of the NCAA tournament.

By the time she completed her college soccer career, Wambach held school records for goals scored (96), game-winning goals (24), assists (49), and points (241). She also ranked as the Division I career leader in points per game (3.17) and goals per game (1.29). She was named Southeastern Conference (SEC) Player of the Year in both 2000 and 2001—becoming the first player ever to claim the honor two years in a row—and was selected as an NCAA All-American three times.

When Wambach left Florida in 2002, she was a few credits short of completing her degree in leisure-services management. But she wanted to take advantage of an exciting opportunity to continue playing soccer in a newly formed professional league, the Women's United Soccer Association (WUSA). "I didn't realize until late in my college career that it was actually something I could do after college, maybe for a living and as a career," she recalled. "Even then, you still had to be the best in the world."

CAREER HIGHLIGHTS

Professional Soccer—The WUSA

Wambach was selected with the second overall pick in the 2002 WUSA draft by the Washington Freedom. She joined a team that was led by one of the legends of women's soccer—Mia Hamm. Wambach considered Hamm a mentor and felt that playing alongside the veteran helped her polish her skills. Although both Hamm and Wambach were known as goal-scorers, their styles of play were very different. Hamm was a small, fast, elusive striker who usually dribbled around opponents to score goals. Wambach, on the other hand, was a tall, physical, high-leaping striker who usually scored after receiving passes in front of the opponent's goal. "She is a mass of woman," said fellow WUSA player Brandi Chastain. "You can't move her very easily, and once she gains position, it's almost impossible to get around her."

Wambach turned in a phenomenal rookie season, leading the Freedom in goals (10), assists (9), and points (29). She was selected to play in the All-Star Game and was named Most Valuable Player (MVP) in that contest, and she easily won the league's Rookie of the Year Award. "I feel like I'm still in the middle of this tornado that's just struck in terms of my career just taking off," she said.

Wambach had an even better year in 2003. She scored 13 goals, added 7 assists, and tied with Hamm for the league lead in scoring with 33 points. The formidable offensive duo took the Freedom all the way to the WUSA championship, known as the Founders Cup. Wambach scored both of her team's goals in the final match, including the game-winner in sudden-death overtime, and was named MVP of the tournament. Unfortunately, the WUSA went out of business just a few weeks after the Freedom's triumph in the 2003 Founders Cup. The fledgling league simply did not attract enough fans and sponsorship money to continue operating. Its failure put an end to women's professional soccer in the United States for six years.

"She is a mass of woman,"
said fellow WUSA player
Brandi Chastain. "You can't
move her very easily, and
once she gains position, it's
almost impossible to get
around her."

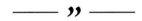

International Soccer—The U.S. Women's National Team

The demise of the WUSA was a big disappointment for Wambach. During her short-lived pro soccer career, however, she also got an opportunity to play for the U.S. Women's National Team (WNT). The WNT would play in the FIFA Women's World Cup, held every four years beginning in 1991, and the Olympic Games, held every four years including 1996. Both of these international events are tournaments with a series of games, with teams eliminated along the way, that lead up to a final match for first place. Led by such well-known players as Mia Hamm, Julie Foudy, Joy Fawcett, Michelle Akers, and Kristine Lilly, the American squad had won the first-ever FIFA Women's World Cup tournament in 1991 and had also earned a gold medal in the 1996 Olympics. Team USA's memorable defeat of China in the 1999 World Cup final—an event watched by 90,185 fans (a world record for a women's sporting event) at the Rose Bowl in California—had also given a big boost to girls' soccer programs all across the United States.

When Wambach was invited to play with the WNT in 2002, she was thrilled to take the field with some of her childhood heroes. Despite scoring five goals in her first seven international matches, however, she was left off the

*Wambach (left) moves the ball around a German defender
at the 2003 Women's World Cup semifinal match.*

WNT roster in spring 2003. Coach April Heinrichs told her that she needed to improve her fitness and play with greater intensity if she hoped to make the team for the 2003 World Cup tournament that fall. "She needed to put it in black-and-white terms for me, and I think a light bulb went off in my head," Wambach remembered. "I wasn't playing my best soccer when I had this talk with April and we both knew it. But I knew something April didn't know—that I was going to start playing better."

Wambach worked hard over the next few months, and her commitment paid off during her tremendous 2003 WUSA championship season. Impressed by her MVP performance in the Founders Cup, Heinrichs selected Wambach as a member of the American team that would compete for the 2003 FIFA Women's World Cup. She appeared in her first World Cup match—a 3-1 U.S. victory over Sweden—on September 21, 2003. Two days later she scored her first World Cup goal in a 5-0 win over Nigeria. She scored again in Team USA's next match, a 3-0 victory over North Korea, and tallied her third goal of the tournament in the WNT's 1-0 victory over Norway in the quarterfinals. Unfortunately, the American squad lost to eventual champion Germany 3-0 in the semifinals. This defeat was a big blow to Wambach and the other American players. Wambach, however, was able to take pride in the fact that she was named U.S. Soccer's Female Athlete of the Year in recognition of her outstanding performance.

Winning an Olympic Gold Medal

Following the disappointing conclusion of the 2003 Women's World Cup, Wambach was determined to capture a gold medal at the 2004 Summer Olympics in Athens, Greece. Her mission gained even more importance when three of the biggest stars of American women's soccer—Mia Hamm, Joy Fawcett, and Julie Foudy—announced that they planned to retire afterward. The WNT spent seven months training together in preparation for the Olympic tournament, and Wambach relished every moment she spent with her legendary teammates. "Every time they talk on the soccer field, I'm listening," she noted. "I just want to absorb as much information from them as I possibly can. If I don't, I'll be cheating myself and the rest of the future of this team."

"I don't think you'd ever use a word like timid about Abby," said teammate Mia Hamm. "She just kind of embraces life and goes for it and doesn't apologize for it. From that standpoint, every single day is high speed with Abby, and it is infectious. It gave us older players that youthful enthusiasm that carried us through."

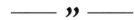

As the Olympic tournament got underway, Wambach once again proved to be a dangerous scoring threat. She scored a goal in each of the first two matches to help the United States defeat Greece 3-0 and Brazil 2-0. She also received yellow cards (penalties) in both contests, however, which meant that she had to sit out the third match against Australia. Her teammates struggled to a 1-1 tie without her. Team USA still advanced to the quarterfinals, where Wambach scored her third goal of the tournament to help beat Japan 2-1. After defeating Germany 2-1 in the semifinals, the American women squared off against Brazil in the gold medal match.

The United States and Brazil played an intense, evenly matched game. With the score deadlocked at 1-1 at the end of regulation time, the two teams were forced to play a 30-minute overtime period. In the 22nd minute, Kristine Lilly lofted a corner kick toward the front of Brazil's goal. Wambach jostled for position and headed the ball into the net. It was her fourth goal of the tournament, and it turned out to be the game-winner for the United States. It was especially meaningful for Wambach to help send her star teammates into retirement with a gold medal. "To be able to play, to be able to win a gold medal, to be able to score the winning goal in the gold-medal game for these women, the women who have given me my way of life, who have given me my job in a lot of respects.... This is the best thank you I could give them," she stated. "It's a dream come true."

Wambach's teammates were eager to give her credit for lifting the United States to victory. "I don't think you'd ever use a word like timid about Abby," said Hamm. "She just kind of embraces life and goes for it and doesn't apologize for it. From that standpoint, every single day is high speed with Abby, and it is infectious. It gave us older players that youthful enthusiasm that carried us through." By the end of 2004, Wambach had scored 31 goals in 30 international matches—the highest per-game average in history. In honor of her remarkable Olympic performance, she earned the U.S. Soccer Female Athlete of the Year Award for the second straight year.

Emerging as the Team Leader

Once the longtime leaders of the WNT retired, Wambach emerged as the top player for the American squad. "Mia was the one. Now Abby's the one," Lilly explained. "Now they're going to be gunning for her." Despite getting more attention from opposing defenses, however, Wambach continued to perform well against international competition. During the 2005 season she scored 4 goals and added 5 assists in the 8 games in which she played. The following year she led Team USA in scoring with 17 goals and 8 assists. Her two most important goals came in a North American regional qualifying victory over Mexico. The win enabled the American squad to qualify for the 2007 FIFA Women's World Cup tournament.

In the first round of the World Cup tournament, Wambach scored a goal as Team USA battled North Korea to a 2-2 tie. In some respects the American squad was relieved to manage a tie, because they did not have Wambach for a significant stretch of the game. She collided with an opposing player midway through and sustained a cut on her head that required 11 stitches. While she was getting patched up in the locker room, she could not wait to return to action. "I was yelling at the doctors to get it done quicker," she remembered. "I cursed some bad words and hurried up and got my jersey on and ran as fast as I could."

Three days later Wambach scored both American goals in a 2-0 victory over Sweden. After Team USA defeated Nigeria 2-1 to reach the quarterfinals, she scored her fourth goal of the tournament to help the American squad beat England 3-0. In the semifinals, however, Wambach and her teammates were shut out by Brazil 4-0 to dash their hopes for a World Cup championship. It was the worst-ever defeat for the WNT. Although Wambach came back to score 2 more goals to help Team USA win the con-

During this game against North Korea in the 2007 Women's World Cup, Wambach cut her head while colliding with another player, left the field to get 11 stitches, and then returned to the game.

solation game against Norway—giving her 6 goals in 6 matches—she was still deeply disappointed in the result. At the end of the year, she received U.S. Soccer Player of the Year honors for the third time.

In 2008 the WNT played 22 games in preparation for the Olympic Games in Beijing, China. Wambach led the team with 13 goals and 10 assists during that period. In Team USA's last exhibition match before the Olympic tournament, however, she crashed into Brazilian defender Andréia Rosa and broke two bones in her leg. Wambach knew right away that the injury was serious. "My knee was pointing up and my foot was pointing in a little bit of a different direction," she explained. The following day she underwent surgery to insert a titanium rod in her leg.

The injury forced Wambach to miss the Olympics. Yet she felt confident that her teammates would prevail in her absence. "I wasn't freaked out about what was ahead, what was in store for the team," she declared. "Yes, I know I'm a very important player for the team. But in the moment, it made me realize even more how insignificant one player is in a team environment. It really does take a team to win championships. There is no doubt in my heart, no doubt in my mind, no doubt in my soul this team can win a gold medal." True to her prediction, Team USA defeated Brazil in the finals to claim the gold medal.

Heading for the World Cup

After nearly a year of recovery and rehabilitation, Wambach returned to international competition in 2009. On July 19 she scored her 100th career goal in international play during a 1-0 victory over Canada in her hometown of Rochester. The milestone placed her behind only Mia Hamm (with 158 career goals) and Kristine Lilly (with 129) on the all-time list of American scorers. By the end of 2010 she had scored 117 goals in 149 international games, a tally that gave her the best goals-per-game ratio in U.S. history. Perhaps most amazingly, 46 of those goals (nearly 40 percent) were struck with her head rather than her feet. Wambach was widely considered to be the best "header" in the world—male or female.

Wambach also returned to professional soccer in 2009 in the newly created Women's Professional Soccer (WPS) league. She joined her old WUSA team, the Washington Freedom, late in the season but still managed to score 8 goals, including 3 game-winners. During the 2010 season Wambach netted 13 goals, including 5 game-winners. Prior to the start of the 2011 season, the Freedom franchise moved to Florida and was renamed magicJack (after the data storage device company that served as its main sponsor). Wambach scored 4 goals in 5 games before leaving to join the WNT in preparation for the FIFA Women's World Cup.

As the 2011 World Cup tournament approached, Wambach desperately wanted to bring home a trophy to make up for the disappointments of 2003 and 2007. "My career will not be complete without a World Cup championship," she declared. "I take it personally that I haven't won one, and I'll be heartbroken if we walk away without one."

At the same time, though, Wambach realized that her role on the team was beginning to change. Under new head coach Pia Sundhage, the WNT moved to a possession-oriented, ball-control offense that emphasized short passes. The team thus moved away from the long passes that had set up many of Wambach's goals over the years. Under the new style, Wambach only scored 1 goal in 10 games in 2011 leading up to the World Cup tournament. "I'm not going to sit here and say I don't want to score," she said. "What I'm going to say is that I would prefer winning to scoring. I've been fortunate to score many goals in the World Cup, and we haven't won one. So I'll set up goals. If I have to watch my teammates score goals and we win the championship, I couldn't care less."

At the 2011 World Cup tournament, Wambach wanted to bring home a trophy to make up for the disappointments of 2003 and 2007. "My career will not be complete without a World Cup championship," she declared. "I take it personally that I haven't won one, and I'll be heartbroken if we walk away without one."

Falling Short in the Final Match

The United States opened the 2011 World Cup tournament with a 2-0 win against North Korea and followed up with a 3-0 victory over Colombia. In the third match, however, Team USA lost 2-1 to Sweden. Wambach broke her scoring drought in that game by putting the ball into the net off her shoulder in the 67th minute of play. But the loss meant that the United States faced a tough quarterfinal matchup against Brazil—the team that had knocked the American women out of contention for the 2007 World Cup.

The United States jumped out to an early lead when Brazilian defender Daiane deflected the ball into her own goal. In the 68th minute, however,

During the 2011 Women's World Cup game against France, the score was tied 1-1 when Wambach headed the ball off a corner kick past France's goalkeeper.

U.S. defender Rachel Buehler received a red card for fouling Brazilian star Marta, the five-time FIFA Player of the Year. Marta made the penalty kick to tie the score at 1-1, and Team USA was forced to play shorthanded (10 players vs. 11) for the remainder of the game. When Marta scored again 2 minutes into the 30-minute overtime period, it appeared as if the U.S. team might endure another early exit from the World Cup tournament. But with time running out, Wambach took a crossing pass from teammate Megan Rapinoe and headed it into Brazil's goal to tie the score 2-2 and force a shootout. All 5 American kickers scored, while U.S. goalkeeper Hope Solo made a key save against the third Brazilian kicker, Daiane, to preserve the epic, come-from-behind victory.

Team USA thus advanced to face France in the semifinals. The score was tied 1-1 until the 79th minute of play, when Wambach scored another header off a corner kick from Lauren Cheney. The United States went on to win 3-1 to advance to the World Cup finals for the first time since 1999. "We've achieved our goal. We're in the final," Wambach said afterward.

"We want to complete it. We want to be world champs." Many Americans felt optimistic about the WNT's chances in the final when they learned that the opponent would be Japan, which was winless against the United States in 25 matches.

Wambach and her teammates came out strong and played some of their best soccer of the tournament against Japan. Although the Americans had dozens of great scoring opportunities, they did not get a goal until the 69th minute on a tough shot by Alex Morgan. The Japanese came right back to tie the score 12 minutes later following a defensive mistake by the U.S. squad. Wambach finally worked her way free of the smothering Japanese defense to score yet another header in the 104th minute of play. It was her fourth goal of the tournament and the 13th World Cup goal of her career, which placed her third on the all-time list. Japan refused to give up, however, and evened the score at 2-2 just a few minutes later. The World Cup championship was ultimately decided in a shootout, which Japan won 3-1. Wambach was the only American shooter to make her penalty shot. For her outstanding performance, she received the Silver Ball Award as the second-best player in the tournament (behind Japan's Homare Sawa) and the Bronze Boot Award as the third-leading goal scorer.

Despite the accolades, Wambach was devastated by the loss. "There are really no words. We were so close," she stated. "Obviously, we wanted to bring home the Cup; we felt we played well enough to do that. Obviously, the Japanese proved to be stronger-willed in the end." Upon returning home to the United States, Wambach and her teammates were gratified to find hundreds of fans waiting to greet them at the airport in New York. The crowds were cheering and waving American flags. "It brought my spirits up more than anything could have," she acknowledged. "I'm so disappointed for my teammates, myself, I'm so disappointed for our country because I really feel we had it, and it was so close. Coming home to this type of reception is truly one of the best things that ever happened."

Planning Ahead

In the immediate future, Wambach plans to remain with the WNT to train for the 2012 Olympic Games in London, England. "London's going to be fantastic, we've just got to qualify," she noted. She also hopes to continue playing professional soccer, but the future of both her magicJack team and the overall WPS appear to be in doubt. Although attendance at games increased following the dramatic Women's World Cup tournament, the league still faces financial problems that threaten its existence.

When her soccer career concludes—most likely following the 2012 Olympics—Wambach hopes to continue reaching out to people internationally. "I want to travel the world in a different capacity," she explained. "Not as a soccer player but as a humanitarian, a philanthropist. I want to own restaurants, own real estate, stuff that I'm working now to afford and achieve."

HOME AND FAMILY

Wambach, who is single, lives in Hermosa Beach, California. She shares her home with a skateboard-riding English bulldog named Kingston.

HOBBIES AND OTHER INTERESTS

In her spare time, Wambach enjoys listening to music, playing video games, surfing, mountain biking, and camping.

HONORS AND AWARDS

High School All-American: 1996, 1997
National High School Player of the Year (NSCAA): 1997
SEC Player of the Year: 2000, 2001
NCAA All-American: 1998, 1999, 2000, 2001
WUSA Rookie of the Year: 2002
WUSA Founders Cup Champion: 2003 (with Washington Freedom)
WUSA Founders Cup MVP: 2003
U.S. Soccer Female Athlete of the Year: 2003, 2004, 2007, 2010
Olympic Women's Soccer: 2004, gold medal (with U.S. Women's National
    Team)
FIFA World Cup Silver Ball: 2011
FIFA World Cup Bronze Boot: 2011

FURTHER READING

Periodicals

Current Biography Yearbook, 2011
Houston Chronicle, July 14, 2011, Sports, p.1
New York Times, July 8, 2007, p.L8; July 17, 2011, p.L1; July 18, 2011, p.D1;
    Aug. 9, 2011, p.B11
Newsday, July 19, 2011
Sports Illustrated, Oct. 1, 2007
Sports Illustrated for Kids, Sep. 2011, p.13
St. Louis Post-Dispatch, July 6, 2011
USA Today, Sep. 18, 2003, p.C10; July 8, 2005, p.C10; June 6, 2011, p.C2; July
    7, 2011, p.C1; July 13, 2011, p.C1

Online Articles

soccernet.espn.go.com
  (ESPN, "Wambach Leads by Example," Aug. 12, 2004)
www.topics.nytimes.com
  (New York Times, "Abby Wambach," multiple articles, various dates)
www.democratandchronicle.com
  (Rochester Democrat-Chronicle, "Abby Wambach Eager to Win a World
  Cup," June 28, 2011)
content.usatoday.com/topics/index
  (USA Today, "Abby Wambach," multiple articles, various dates)

ADDRESS

Abby Wambach
U.S. Soccer Federation
1801 South Prairie Avenue
Chicago, IL 60616

WEB SITES

www.abbywambach.com
www.ussoccer.com/teams/wnt/abby-wambach
www.gatorzone.com/soccer/bios

Photo and Illustration Credits

Front Cover photos: Rob Bell: Courtesy of Rob Bell and Mars Hill Bible Church; Michele Norris: © NPR 2007 by Steven Voss; Emma Stone: Jim Spellman/WireImage; Abby Wambach: Carmen Jaspersen/EPA/Landov.

Rob Bell/Photos: Courtesy of Rob Bell and Mars Hill Bible Church (pp. 9, 11, 12); Romain Blanquart/MTC/Landov (p. 14); DVD cover: RAIN © 2002 Nooma. © 2005 by Flannel.org. Published by Zondervan. All rights reserved. (p. 17); Courtesy of Rob Bell and Mars Hill Bible Church (p. 20).

Big Time Rush/Photos: AP Photo/Seth Wenig (p. 25); PRNewsFoto/Nickelodeon, Stewart Shining/via Newscom (p. 27); PRNewsFoto/Nickelodeon, Ben Watts/via Newscom (p. 30); CD cover: BIG TIME RUSH © 2010 Nickelodeon/Columbia/Sony Music Entertainment (p. 33); Kevork Djansezian/Getty Images for Nickelodeon/KCA2011 (p. 35).

Cheryl Burke/Photos: FayesVision/WENN.com/Newscom (p. 37); ABC/Craig Sjodin (p. 41); Adam Larkey/ABC via Getty Images (p. 42); ABC/Adam Taylor (p. 46).

Josh Hamilton/Photos: John Sleezer/MCT/Landov (p. 49); AP Photo/St. Petersburg Times/Jonathan Newton (p. 52); Ezra Shaw/Getty Images (p. 54); AP Photo/Rusty Kennedy (p. 58); Ron Jenkins/Fort Worth Star-Telegram/MCT via Getty Images (p. 61); AP Photo/Jeff Roberson (p. 63).

Bruno Mars/Photos: Jason Merritt/Getty Images (p. 67); Catherine McGann/Getty Images (p. 69); PRNewsFoto/Renaissance Hotels via AP (p. 70); CD cover: DOO-WOPS & HOOLIGANS © 2010 NEK/New Elektra/Warner Atlantic Elektra Corporation (p. 73); John Shearer/WireImage (p. 76).

Stella McCartney/Photos: EPA Photo/EPA/Hugo Philpot/Newscom (p. 79); David Montgomery/Getty Images (p. 81); AP Photo/Michel Euler (p. 84); Eric Ryan/Getty Images (p. 87); Photos from the Winter 2011 Collection, Stella McCartney.com (p. 89).

Blake Mycoskie/Photos: Donato Sardella/WireImage (p. 93); Tony Esparza/CBS/Landov (p. 95); AP Photo/Ali Burafi (p. 98); PRNewsFoto/TOMS Shoes/via Newscom (p. 100); Michael Kovac/Getty Images for TOMS (p. 103).

Michele Norris/Photos: © NPR 2007 by Steven Voss (p. 107); Photo by Russell Lee, FSO/OWI Photograph Collection, Library of Congress, LC-USF3301-012327-M5 (p. 109); Courtesy, Michele Norris (pp. 111, 113, 116); Book cover: THE GRACE OF SILENCE © 2010 by Michele Norris. All rights reserved. Published by Vintage Books

Cumulative Names Index

This cumulative index includes the names of all individuals profiled in *Biography Today* since the debut of the series in 1992.

For cumulative general, places of birth, and birthday indexes, please see biographytoday.com.

165

For cumulative general, places of birth, and birthday indexes, please see biographytoday.com.

167

For cumulative general, places of birth, and birthday indexes, please see biographytoday.com.

169

   For cumulative general, places of birth, and birthday indexes, please see biographytoday.com.

For cumulative general, places of birth, and birthday indexes, please see biographytoday.com.

For cumulative general, places of birth, and birthday indexes, please see biographytoday.com.

For cumulative general, places of birth, and birthday indexes, please see biographytoday.com.

177

For cumulative general, places of birth, and birthday indexes, please see biographytoday.com.

179

For cumulative general, places of birth, and birthday indexes, please see biographytoday.com.

Biography Today

General Series

Biography Today **General Series** includes a unique combination of current biographical profiles that teachers and librarians — and the readers themselves — tell us are most appealing. The **General Series** is available as a 3-issue subscription; hardcover annual cumulation; or subscription plus cumulation.

Within the **General Series**, your readers will find a variety of sketches about:

- Authors
- Musicians
- Political leaders
- Sports figures
- Movie actresses & actors
- Cartoonists
- Scientists
- Astronauts
- TV personalities
- and the movers & shakers in many other fields!

ONE-YEAR SUBSCRIPTION
- 3 softcover issues, 6" x 9"
- Published in January, April, and September
- 1-year subscription, list price $66. **School and library price $64**
- 150 pages per issue
- 10 profiles per issue
- Contact sources for additional information
- Cumulative Names Index

HARDBOUND ANNUAL CUMULATION
- Sturdy 6" x 9" hardbound volume
- Published in December
- List price $73. **School and library price $66 per volume**
- 450 pages per volume
- 30 profiles — includes all profiles found in softcover issues for that calendar year
- Cumulative General Index, Places of Birth Index, and Birthday Index

SUBSCRIPTION AND CUMULATION COMBINATION
- $110 for 3 softcover issues plus the hardbound volume

For Cumulative General, Places of Birth, and Birthday Indexes, please see www.biographytoday.com.

"*Biography Today* will be useful in elementary and middle school libraries and in public library children's collections where there is a need for biographies of current personalities. High schools serving reluctant readers may also want to consider a subscription."
— *Booklist,* American Library Association

"Highly recommended for the young adult audience. Readers will delight in the accessible, energetic, tell-all style; teachers, librarians, and parents will welcome the clever format [and] intelligent and informative text. It should prove especially useful in motivating 'reluctant' readers or literate nonreaders."
— *MultiCultural Review*

"Written in a friendly, almost chatty tone, the profiles offer quick, objective information. While coverage of current figures makes *Biography Today* a useful reference tool, an appealing format and wide scope make it a fun resource to browse." — *School Library Journal*

"The best source for current information at a level kids can understand."
— Kelly Bryant, School Librarian, Carlton, OR

"Easy for kids to read. We love it! Don't want to be without it."
— Lynn McWhirter, School Librarian, Rockford, IL